First Certificate

writing SKILLS

D1412144

Nelson

Peter Anderson

elson (Hong Kong) Ltd
an Building 10/F
A Westlands Road
Quarry Bay Hong Kong

© Peter Anderson 1987

First published by Unwin Hyman Limited 1987
(Under ISBN 0 7135 2588 6)

Reprinted once
Second impression published by Thomas Nelson and Sons Ltd 1989

ISBN 0-17-555812-4
NPN 9 8 7 6 5

All rights reserved. No part of this publication may be reproduced, copied or transmitted save with written permission or in accordance with the provisions of the Copyright, Design and Patents Act 1988, or under the terms of any licence permitting limited copying issued by the Copyright Licensing Agency, 90 Tottenham Court Road, London, W1P 9HE.

Any person who does any unauthorised act in relation to this publication may be liable to criminal prosecution and civil claims for damages.

Designed by Wendi Watson

Typeset by August Filmsetting, Haydock, St Helens
Printed and bound in Hong Kong

Acknowledgements

Illustrations by Liz Inwood (pp. 22 and 50) and Lisa Folland (p. 33)

The publishers are grateful to the following for permission to reproduce copyright material. They have tried to contact all copyright holders but where they have failed will be pleased to make the necessary arrangements at the first opportunity.

Sheffield City Council for the poster on p.11; the National Union of Teachers for the materials on p. 17; the London Cycling Campaign and the London Borough of Camden for the advertisements on p.18; the Ipswich Parachute Centre for the advertisement on p. 24; Sport Aid for the leaflet on p. 31; Eurocamp for the advertisement on p. 42; Action Aid for the advertisement on p. 46; Windsor Safari Park for the materials on p. 55; CBS Records for the poster on p. 61; HM Customs and Excise for the leaflet on p. 76; Warwick Castle for the advertisement on p. 91; Penguin Books for the book cover on p. 92; the estate of the late Sonia Brownwell Orwell and Secker and Warburg for the extract from *Nineteen Eighty-Four* on p. 93; the Royal Shakespeare Company for the poster of their production of *Romeo and Juliet* at the Aldwych Theatre, 1981, on p. 95.

Photographs
Rex Features for p. 4; the Associated Press for pp. 15, 35, 79 and 82; Sally and Richard Greenhill for p. 19; Citroën and Volkswagen for p. 25; Barnaby's for pp. 31, 40, 56 (the 2nd), 60 and 70; the Scottish Tourist Board for p. 65; Camera Press for pp. 85 and 86; Brian Shuel for p. 87.

Contents

1 Informal letters (1)

PRESENTATION

Read the following letter, in which Dave invites Alan to a fancy-dress party.

LETTER 1

25, Long Lane
Marsden
MN5 6OB
3rd June 1987

Dear Alan,

Sorry I haven't written to you for such a long time, but I've been revising hard for my final exams and so just haven't been able to find the time. I'm sure you know what it's like!

Anyway, the last exam is on Friday, June 19th, so we've decided to celebrate by holding a fancy-dress party at the house on the Saturday evening. The theme of the party is "The Movies" and I'm thinking of going either as Humphrey Bogart or John Wayne! So, if you haven't got anything arranged for that weekend, why not grab a costume and come over to Marsden? It'd be great to see you again!

I've drawn a map showing you how to get here from the Station so that you don't get lost. It's very easy to find. You can either walk – about 15 minutes – or take a number 74 bus from outside Marks and Spencer's. If you decide to get the bus, get off at the Black Swan pub and walk down Swallowfield Avenue, which leads into Long Lane.

Well, that's all for now. I think I'd better get back to my revision. Hope to see you in two weeks' time.

Yours
Dave

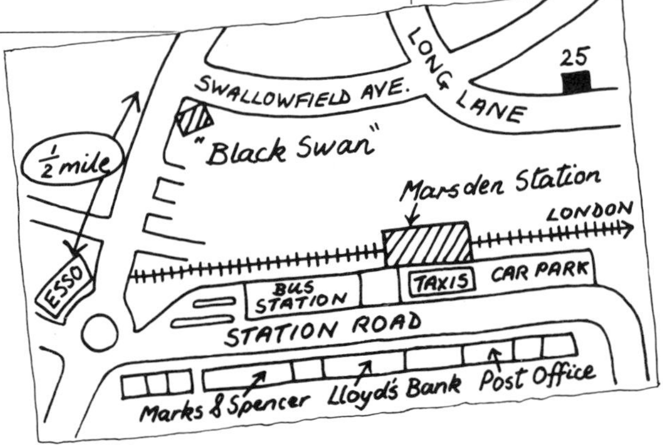

ANALYSIS

Comprehension check

1 *Using the* underlined *words to help you, complete the following sentences about the letter.*

a Dave hasn't had the time to write to Alan because ....

....

b He and his friends are having a party because ....

....

c He has sent Alan a map to ....

....

2 *Mark the position on the map of the following:*

a Dave's house
b where Alan should get on the bus
c where Alan should get off the bus

Layout

Look at Letter 1 again and at this diagram. Notice the position of each part of the letter.

Unscramble the words below and then use them to write the beginning of a letter to John.

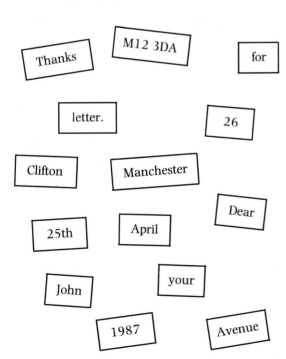

Thanks
M12 3DA
for
letter.
26
Clifton
Manchester
Dear
25th
April
John
your
1987
Avenue

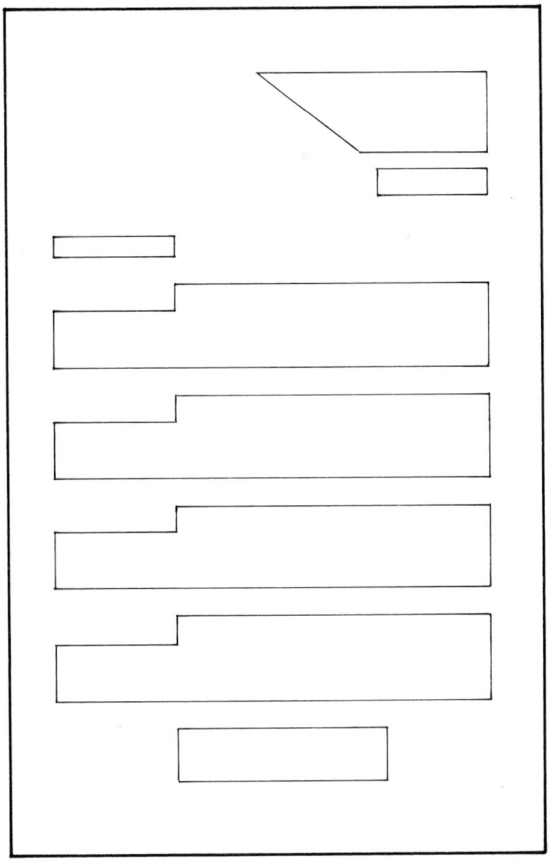

Text organisation

There are four paragraphs in Dave's letter to Alan.
Complete the following summary of each paragraph.

Paragraph 1 Dave apologises for not writing ....
and explains that ....

Paragraph 2 He tells Alan that they are having a fancy-dress party and ....
....

Paragraph 3 He explains ....

Paragraph 4 He closes the letter by saying that he must ....
.... and that he hopes ....

Why does Dave begin a new paragraph each time?

ANALYSIS

Text organisation

First read the letter on the right and then, in pairs, decide how it should be divided into paragraphs.

LETTER 2

Dear Jane, thanks for your letter, which took an incredible ten days to get here! It was lovely to hear all the news from England. Congratulations on passing your driving test (at last!). I hope you haven't run any old ladies over yet! No, joking apart, I'm glad you've passed your test because now you'll be able to teach me to drive when I come home next month. Well, the time's really flying by here! It's hard to believe I've been here in France nearly six weeks now. Fortunately, 'les enfants terribles' (the kids) have gone to stay with their grandparents in the country so I've got a lot more free time now. Yesterday I spent almost the whole day sunbathing on the beach with Maria, a Spanish au-pair that I've made friends with. As you can imagine, I'm getting a really good tan, though I still look white compared with Maria. By the way, could you do me a favour? Maria's sister, Elena, will be coming to England at the beginning of August to study English. She'll be staying with an English family in Cambridge for six weeks. As she doesn't know anybody in Cambridge, I was wondering if you could meet up with her one day and show her round. The phone number is 742316. You needn't worry about having to speak Spanish to her because Maria says her English is pretty good. Right, I had better start getting the lunch ready. (Snails again!) Give my love to all at home. Write again soon.

Love, Tina

Useful language

Now look again at Letter 1 and Letter 2.

Which words or expressions do the writers use to show that they are going to change the topic of conversation? These are usually used at the beginning of a new paragraph.

e.g. **Anyway** (Letter 1, Paragraph 2)

Linking ideas

1 Below is the opening paragraph of a letter.

In pairs, discuss how you think this paragraph could be improved.

First write a new version of the paragraph and then compare it with the first paragraph of Letter 1.

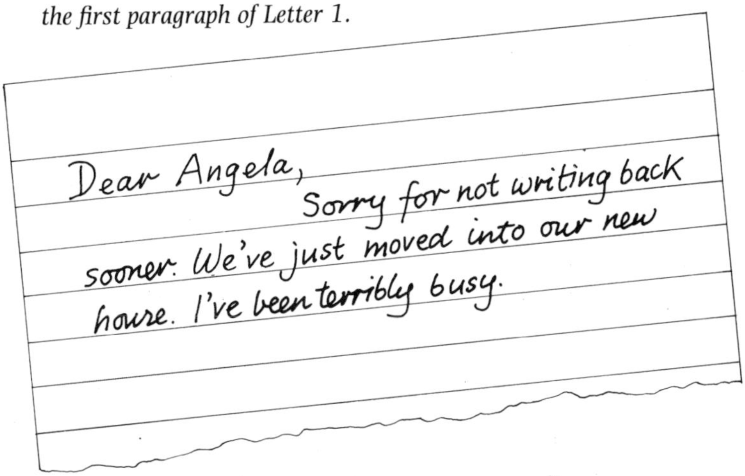

Dear Angela,
Sorry for not writing back
sooner. We've just moved into our new
house. I've been terribly busy.

2 *Using the* underlined *words to help you, complete the following sentences about Tina's letter to Jane.*

1 Jane's letter took .... France.

2 She has more free time at the moment because ....

....

3 She's getting a very good suntan but ....

....

4 Elena is going to England because ....

5 She speaks English well so ....

PRACTICE

Exercise 1

In pairs, re-write the following letter, using the words in brackets to help you.
Pay special attention to the following:

LAYOUT Are the address, date and salutation correct and in the right position?
STRUCTURE Is it divided into paragraphs in the appropriate places?
STYLE Are the ideas linked together by suitable connectors?

Note that when using a connector to link sentences together, you will sometimes need to omit certain words (as in the example below) or change the tense of a verb.

Gerald and Eileen Swain
request the pleasure of the company of
Mark and Susan
at the marriage of their daughter
Katherine
with
Mr Anthony Williams
at The University Church of St. Mary the Virgin, Oxford
on Saturday, 29th August, 1987 at 12.00 p.m.
and afterwards at The Randolph Hotel, Oxford

79 Church Row
Oxford
OX1 2BR

R.S.V.P.

LETTER 3

Mark Crawford
Shakespeare Gardens, 22
N2 6RZ London, 4th May 1987

Hello Tony! Hello Kate!

1 Thanks for the invitation to your wedding. It arrived this morning. (which) Many congratulations! **2** I must admit it was a bit of a surprise. You've been living together for over five years now. (as)
3 Unfortunately, we've booked a holiday in Ibiza. It starts the same day as your wedding. I'm afraid we won't be able to make it. (which, so)
4 I phoned the travel agent's immediately. I tried to get them to change the dates. They told me that all the hotels were fully booked until September. (to, but) **5** Anyway, send me your wedding list. We can get you a present. (so that) Now, I've got some good news of my own. **6** I went for an interview yesterday for a job as a sales manager. They offered it to me there and then. (and) **7** I was so surprised. At first, I didn't know what to say. (so ... that)
8 Anyway, they've given me until next weekend. Then I have to make up my mind. (to) **9** The work sounds very interesting. The salary's excellent. They've offered me a company car. (and) However, there's just one little snag. **10** The job would be based in Brighton. I'd have to commute from London every day. It would be extremely tiring. It would also be rather expensive. (so, which, and) **11** But I think it would be an excellent opportunity for me. I've decided to accept the job. (so) **12** Right, I'd better finish now. I want to catch the last post. (so) Hope to see you both before the wedding.

Goodbye,
Mark

e.g. Thanks for the invitation to your wedding, **which** arrived this morning.

Exercise 2

First read the letter below and then fill in the gaps and write a suitable last paragraph.

LETTER 4

Dear Mandy,

.... I wasn't able to come to your party last weekend .... I had to ....

Unfortunately, ...

.................................., I was wondering if .... favour. You know I applied for a job with .... a few weeks ago. .... , believe it or not, they want me to come .... in London next .... The problem is that it's first thing in the morning, at nine o'clock, ... I'd have to leave Warwick at half-past five in the morning .... interview in time .... I'd be quite tired by the time I arrived.

So, do you think .... at your flat on Wednesday night .... I can get a good night's sleep before the interview. Don't worry about .... a bed for me. I can sleep anywhere – on a sofa, on the floor (or even in the bath!). Also I'd bring my own sleeping-bag, ... you wouldn't have to provide any .... or ....

....
....
....

....

Debby

GUIDED WRITING

Composition task

Below are two extracts from the diary of Jo-Ellen, an American girl who has gone to Rome to study Italian. She is staying with an Italian family, the Rossi's, who live at:

Via Bruzzesi, 29
00196 Roma
Italy

Imagine that you are Jo-Ellen. Use the information in the diary to form the main part of a letter she writes to Barbara, a friend of hers. You will need to use your imagination to write the beginning and the ending. (See Letter 1 and Letter 2.) Date the letter 21st June 1987 and write between 120 and 180 words.

LETTER 5

JUNE 1987 Monday 15

Moved in with Italian family – the Rossi's – mid 40's – two children – Paola (14), Gabriella (19). They're all very hospitable. Great room with fantastic view over St. Peter's. Swimming-pool in garden! Weather extremely hot and sticky – probably spend all my free time in the pool! None of the family speak English – Guess I'll have to speak Italian all the time! Party with Gabriella Saturday.

JUNE 1987 Sunday 21

At the Rossi's a week now. Excellent food but too much – have to make sure I don't put on weight! All went to beach today at Ostia – a bit sunburnt. Party last night at a friend of Gabriella's – barbecue in garden; disco outside; danced for hours; met lots of Gabriella's friends – they all wanted to practise their English – not much chance to speak Italian!

2 Discursive essays (1)

PRESENTATION

Read the following essay about whether public transport in our cities should be free.

ESSAY 1

All public transport in our cities should be free. Discuss.

In most cities public transport is partially subsidised by the city council, which means that bus and underground fares are usually reasonably low. However, some people argue that fares should be abolished altogether. In this essay I intend to examine the arguments for and against free public transport.

One of the strongest arguments in favour of free public transport is that it would encourage more people to use the buses and tubes instead of going by car. Consequently, there would be far less traffic on the roads, which would make our cities safer, cleaner and generally pleasanter places to live in. Another advantage is that those who are not very well off would be able to afford to go out more and would have a little more money to spend, which would improve the quality of their lives. Free public transport would also be a good thing for a city's shops and businesses, as bus and underground users would have more money available to spend on both necessities and luxuries. Lastly, if passengers travelled free on public transport, there would be no need for ticket offices, bus conductors or ticket inspectors. This would make the buses and undergrounds much cheaper to run.

On the other hand, there are several arguments against abolishing fares. To begin with, if there were no fares, the city council would have to find another way of financing public transport, probably by increasing the city's rates*. As a result, a lot of people who never travel by public transport would be helping to pay for a service which they do not use, which many would consider unfair and which would also make these people worse off. What is more, if the number of passengers increased dramatically because of the abolition of fares, it would probably be necessary to increase the number of buses and trains. This would make free public transport even more expensive to operate. Finally, the abolition of fares would lead to the loss of several thousand jobs among those public transport staff who sell or inspect tickets, which is clearly undesirable in these times of high unemployment.

On balance, I am in favour of the idea of free public transport in our cities provided that alternative employment could be found for those workers whose jobs would become redundant.

* local property tax

2

ANALYSIS

Text organisation

There are four paragraphs in Essay 1.

1 *Complete the following summary of each paragraph.*

Paragraph 1 The writer introduces the subject of the essay by explaining that in most cities public transport fares are fairly cheap but that some people think that ....

He/She then tells the reader that ....

Paragraph 2 The writer gives the arguments .... free public transport and explains what the advantages would be.

Paragraph 3 The writer gives .... free public transport and explains what .... would be.

Paragraph 4 The writer concludes the essay by giving his own .... the idea of abolishing fares.

2 *Complete the table below, which shows the organisation of ideas in paragraphs 2 and 3.*

Free public transport			
FOR (Paragraph 2)		AGAINST (Paragraph 3)	
Points	Word or phrase which introduces each point	Points	Word or phrase which introduces each point
1	One of the strongest arguments	1 council would need to pay for it	....
2 less well off could go out more and have more money	....	2 would need to provide more buses and trains	....
3 people would spend more in shops and businesses	....	3	....
4	Lastly		

Linking ideas

Using the underlined *words to help you, complete the following sentences about Essay 1.*

1 Bus and underground fares are fairly cheap in most cities because ....

2 If more people used public transport, ... and our cities ....

3 The quality of poor people's lives would be better because ....

4 If bus and tube users had more money to spend, it would be good for ....

5 Many people who never use the buses or tubes would have to contribute towards the cost of free public transport because the council ....

6 A free public transport system would be even more expensive to run because if there were a lot more passengers, ...

PRACTICE

Exercise 1

First read the following sentences and then fill in the gaps with one of the words below.

1 In the first place, private schools are able to pay higher salaries than state schools. .... , they are able to attract the best teachers.
2 Some people feel strongly that the working week should be reduced to thirty hours. They claim that .... would help create more jobs and result in greater efficiency.
3 Another advantage of encouraging young people to go to universities far from where they live is that it forces them to leave home, ... makes them become more independent.
4 Secondly, some people argue that if boys and girls are educated separately, then they will not be distracted from their studies when they begin to take an interest in the opposite sex. .... , they say, children from single sex-schools usually obtain better exam results than those from mixed schools.
5 It is well known that alcohol slows down the body's reactions, ... means that in general people are worse drivers if they have had something to drink.
6 What is more, if there were more cycle lanes in large towns, more people would cycle to school and to work. .... , there would be fewer cars and less pollution.
7 Also, drivers who always wear seat belts might take more risks because they feel safer in their cars. .... could lead to an increase in the number of road accidents.
8 Another reason why teachers should be paid more is that it would encourage more university graduates to become teachers, ... would probably improve the standard of teaching in our schools.

which   this   as a result   consequently

2

GUIDED WRITING

Essay planning

*In pairs, first consider the following statements and then note down three arguments **for** and **against** each one.*

1 Mothers with young children should not go out to work. Discuss.
2 All nuclear power stations should be closed down. Discuss.
3 Except in cases of medical necessity, abortion should be illegal. Discuss.

FOR	AGAINST
1	1 ....
2	2 ....
3	3 ....

Composition task

Choose one of the essay topics above and write an essay of between 120 and 180 words.

Use the structure suggested below.

ESSAY 2

Paragraph 1 Introduce the subject of the essay. State why it is an important issue at the present time.
Paragraph 2 Give the arguments in favour of the statement.
Paragraph 3 Give the arguments against the statement.
Paragraph 4 Conclude the essay by giving your own opinion on the subject.

ANALYSIS

Text organisation

The sentences in the essay below are in the wrong order.

1 *In pairs, put them in the correct order (1–11) and decide where the essay should be divided into paragraphs.*

ESSAY 3

The death penalty should be re-introduced for terrorists who commit murder. Discuss.

a However, in my opinion the re-introduction of capital punishment would have little or no effect on reducing terrorism. ☐

b A lot of people argue that if the government brought back the death penalty, it would deter terrorists from carrying out their attacks against the army, the police and innocent civilians. ☐

c I am very much opposed to the idea of 'An eye for an eye, a tooth for a tooth'. ☐

d Apart from this we have seen in the past that the death sentence does not usually deter terrorists. ☐

e These people believe that if terrorists knew that they would be hanged for murder and not just sentenced to life imprisonment, they would probably be too frightened to commit their terrible crimes. ☐

f In most Western countries convicted murderers are no longer sentenced to death but are usually given life imprisonment instead. ☐

g In the first place it seems to me that most terrorists are such fanatical people that they would be prepared to die for their cause. ☐

h For example, terrorist attacks against the Spanish security forces were extremely common during the 1960s and early 1970s, even though capital punishment existed in Spain until 1978. ☐

i All things considered, I do not agree with those who say that we ought to bring back the death penalty for terrorists. ☐

j However, during the last twenty years the West has seen a large increase in acts of terrorism and many people now feel strongly that capital punishment should be re-introduced for terrorists who are convicted of murder. ☐

k Finally, I am strongly against capital punishment because I feel that it is morally wrong to take the life of another human being, even if that person has committed murder. ☐

2 *Complete the following analysis of Essay 3.*

Paragraph 1 Introduction to topic – Sentences **f** and ....
Paragraph 2 .... – Sentences .... and ....
Paragraph 3 The writer's opinion – Sentence ....
First point – Sentence **g**
Second point – Sentences .... and **h**
Third point – Sentences .... and ....
Paragraph 4 Conclusion – Sentence ....

3 What are the three arguments supporting the writer's opinion?

4 Which word or phrase does he/she use to introduce each one?

Useful language

STATING OTHER PEOPLE'S OPINIONS A lot of people think/feel/believe that ... Some people say/argue that ... Many people are in favour of/against/ opposed to ...	STATING YOUR OWN OPINIONS I think/feel/believe that ... Personally/In my opinion/In my view ... It seems to me that ... I am (strongly/very much) in favour of/ against/opposed to ...
INTRODUCING POINTS Firstly/In the first place/To begin with ... Secondly/Another advantage/Another reason ... What is more/Besides/Also/In addition/ Moreover/Furthermore ... Apart from this/that ... Finally/Lastly ...	CONCLUDING THE DISCUSSION On balance, I am in favour of ... Personally, ... All things considered, ... To sum up, ... In conclusion, ...

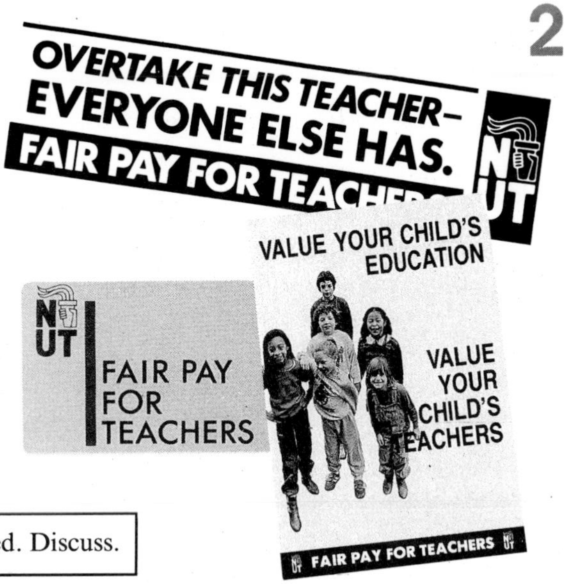

PRACTICE

Exercise 2

*First read the following essay about teachers' salaries and then fill in the gaps with suitable words and phrases from the lists in **Useful language** or with one of the words below:*

ESSAY 4

Teachers' salaries should be substantially increased. Discuss.

Over the last ten years academic standards in our schools have fallen considerably and a lot of people .... that this drop in standards has happened because teachers are so badly paid. .... , many of our best teachers are leaving teaching for better paid jobs in other professions and fewer students now decide to train as teachers when they finish university.

.... that we cannot afford to pay teachers more money as the country is in the middle of an economic recession. These people also .... that although teachers' salaries are not very high, they do not work as many hours as the majority of people.

However, ... my .... the government must find the money to increase teachers' pay for several reasons: .... , it is essential if we wish to keep our best teachers from leaving the profession as well as to encourage our best students to train to become teachers when they finish university. .... would help to raise academic standards once again and would also result in a better educated work force, ... would help the country to come out of its economic recession. .... , I do not agree with those people who .... that teachers have shorter working weeks than other people. Although they may only teach for 25–30 hours a week, most teachers also spend many hours preparing lessons and marking homework. .... , most teachers actually work more hours than people in other professions. .... , I feel that the salary structure for teachers should be changed so that they can get promotion as quickly as in some other professions.

.... , ... teachers' salaries should be increased because it is vitally important to encourage the best people to enter the teaching profession and because teachers work extremely hard and deserve to receive more money.

---

which this as a result consequently

2

GUIDED WRITING

Essay planning

First consider the following statement and decide on your own opinion. Then note down three arguments which other people might use against you and three arguments which support your opinion.

> Large towns should have special lanes for cyclists along all main roads. Discuss.

OTHER PEOPLE'S ARGUMENTS	YOUR ARGUMENTS
1	1 ....
....	....
2	2 ....
....	....
3	3 ....
....	....

Composition task

Use the structure suggested below and write an essay of between 120 and 180 words.

ESSAY 5

Paragraph 1 Introduce the subject of the essay. State why it is an important issue at the present time.
Paragraph 2 Give the arguments which other people (who you do not agree with) might use.
Paragraph 3 Give the arguments which support your own opinion.
Paragraph 4 Conclude the essay by summarising your own opinion in one sentence.

3 Narratives (1)

PRESENTATION

Read the following composition, in which Mary explains how she spent a night on a train during a holiday in Italy.

COMPOSITION 1

The worst night I have ever spent was on a train travelling between Rome and Brindisi, in the south of Italy. It was a hot, sticky night in August and my boyfriend and I had decided to travel overnight on the nine o'clock train so that we could save money by sleeping on the train.

No sooner had we arrived at the station than things started to go wrong. When we joined the queue for tickets it was moving so slowly that we felt sure that we would miss our train. Fortunately, with only two minutes remaining, we managed to buy our tickets and rushed down the platform towards our train.

As soon as we opened the door of the first carriage we realised that this was not going to be a very comfortable journey. The whole carriage, including the corridor, was packed with young soldiers who were obviously travelling to the South to do their military service. With difficulty we made our way down the train until, at last, we found a space in the corridor at the end of the last carriage. Clearly we had a long, uncomfortable night ahead.

By this time it was ten past nine and our train should have left ten minutes before. However, the driver and guard were enjoying a cigarette together on the platform as if they had all the time in the world. When I asked one of the conscripts if he knew why there was a delay he told me that some of the signalmen had gone on strike. Just our luck!

Eventually, just after two o'clock in the morning, the guard blew his whistle. As the train set off, all the soldiers started to cheer and applaud ironically. During our five hour wait we had made friends with several of our military travelling companions and had sung pop songs together to pass the time.

At first, we tried to sleep, using our rucksacks as pillows, but it proved impossible. Every ten to fifteen minutes, just as we were falling asleep, we were woken up by somebody climbing over us to reach the toilet.

In the end we gave up trying to sleep and spent the rest of the night playing cards with the soldiers. I think it was the longest, most exhausting night of my life.

3

ANALYSIS

Ordering events

In pairs, put the following events from Composition 1 in the correct order (1–13), using the words underlined to help you. If two events happened at the same time, indicate this by putting both in the same position.

a	They realised the train was late.	☐
b	They went to the railway station.	☐
c	They found an empty space.	☐
d	The train started moving.	☐
e	The scheduled departure time passed.	☐
f	The soldiers cheered and clapped.	☐
g	They realised the train was very full.	☐
h	They joined the ticket queue.	☐
i	The driver and guard lit their cigarettes.	☐
j	They decided to take the nine o'clock train.	1
k	They got on the train.	☐
l	They walked down the train.	☐
m	They got to know some of the soldiers.	☐

Linking ideas

Find an example in Composition 1 of each of the following connectors and consider how they are used.

and but so that to as until so . . . that
just as no sooner . . . than when as soon as however

If there are any you do not understand, ask your partner or your teacher to explain them to you.

PRACTICE

Exercise 1

Link each of the following pairs of sentences together using one of the connectors opposite.
In some cases you will need to omit certain words and/or change the tense of a verb.

e.g. She walked over to their table. She asked him to dance.
She walked over to their table **and** asked him to dance.

1 The sand was extremely hot. You could not walk on it without any shoes on.
2 The waiter disappeared into the kitchen. They ran out of the restaurant without paying.
3 After the meal they took a taxi to the disco. The man on the door refused to let them in because they were wearing jeans.
4 He went to see his bank manager the following morning. He wanted to ask him if the bank could lend him the money for the sports car.
5 We came out of the restaurant. The car bomb went off a hundred yards down the road.
6 The motorcyclist roared off from the traffic lights. At that very same moment an ambulance went through the red light, coming from the hospital.
7 He took out his binoculars. He wanted to see what the men were doing on the other side of the river.
8 She carried on reading the novel in bed. At midnight she felt too tired to continue and put out the light.

ANALYSIS

Ordering events

a When I **asked** one of the conscripts if he knew why there was a delay he **told** me that some of the signalmen **had gone** on strike. (Paragraph 4)

b As the train **set off**, all the soldiers **started** to cheer and applaud ironically. (Paragraph 5)

c When we **joined** the queue for tickets it **was moving** so slowly that we felt sure we would miss our train. (Paragraph 2)

In the sentences above, put the **highlighted** *verbs in the order in which the actions happened. If you think that two actions happened at the same time, which one started slightly (perhaps a few seconds) before the other?*

a 1 ....
2 ....
3 ....

b 1 ....
2 ....

c 1 ....
2 ....

*Look again at sentences a, b and c above and notice how the past simple (***asked***), past perfect (***had gone***) and past continuous (***was moving***) are used.*

PRACTICE

Exercise 2

First read the following story and then fill in the gaps with one of the verbs below, taking care to use the correct tense.
Some of the verbs may be used more than once.

COMPOSITION 2

During the Second World War, a US aircraft carrier .... (1) the Atlantic towards Europe when the captain .... (2) a radio message from Washington DC which .... (3) him that Seaman Martin's wife had been killed in a car accident.

So he .... (4) the Chief Petty Officer to the bridge and .... (5) him to tell Martin what .... (6). Unfortunately, the Chief Petty Officer was a rather brutal man and .... (7) the news to Martin rather heartlessly:

'Seaman Martin. Attention! Your wife .... (8) last night in a car crash. Dismiss!'

Martin, an extremely sensitive young man, was so upset when he .... (9) this news that he .... (10) himself in his cabin and .... (11) extremely drunk that night.

The next day, when Seaman Martin failed to appear for inspection everybody assumed that he .... (12) suicide by jumping overboard. Naturally, the captain was furious with the CPO:

'If you'd broken the news to him more gently, we wouldn't have lost one of our finest gunners. For God's sake, please try to be a little more diplomatic if this kind of thing happens again.'

Three months later, just as the ship .... (13) at Southampton for essential repairs the port authorities .... (14) the captain that the wife of another sailor, Seaman Henderson, ... (15). Once again, the CPO .... (16) to break the news to the unfortunate man.

This time he .... (17) all of the men up on deck.

'Men. Attention! Right, all those of you who are married take one step forward. Not so fast, Henderson!'

arrive	call	die	hear	lock	ask	commit	get
inform	radio	break	cross	happen	kill	receive	

ANALYSIS

Linking ideas

When narrating we often use connecting phrases such as the four phrases **highlighted** in the passage above. The purpose of these phrases is to indicate when each of the events in a narrative happened.

Look again at Mary's description of her night on the train in Composition 1. Find words or phrases at the beginning of sentences which serve the same purpose. Add them to the list of time connectors below.

First ...	At that moment ...	....
Then/Next ...	During .../Meanwhile ...	....
After/Before (that) ...	The next/following (day) ...	....
Afterwards/Beforehand ...	(Three months) later ...	....
Finally ...	This time ...	....

PRACTICE

Exercise 3

First read the following composition and then fill in the gaps with a variety of suitable time connectors from the list above and put the verbs in brackets in the correct tenses.

COMPOSITION 3

One hot summer's day my father and I (drive) (1) along an extremely narrow country lane in Oxfordshire when we were involved in an awful accident. We (be) (2) to visit my grandmother in a tiny village called Russell's Water and (return) (3) home to Reading.

We (travel) (4) at about thirty-five miles an hour when, all of a sudden, a huge deer (fly) (5) over the hedge and landed with a thud on the bonnet. We stopped the car and jumped out.

.... (6), we thought we (kill) (7) the deer instantly. .... (8) we realised that its eyes were still half open and it was still breathing. .... (9) discussing for several minutes what we should do, it was decided that I should go to the next village to telephone for help while my father stayed with the deer.

Ten minutes .... (10) I arrived breathlessly in the next village, having run most of the way, and found a telephone box. .... (11) I called Directory Enquiries to ask them for the number of a nearby vet. .... (12) I phoned the vet and explained what had happened. He said he would come as soon as he could.

.... (13) the vet (arrive) (14) at the scene of the accident. .... (15) the deer was breathing very slowly. .... (16) he (examine) (17) it carefully the vet (sigh) (18) and said that the most humane thing to do was to put it out of its misery.

He opened his bag and took out a syringe. .... (19) he filled the syringe with a dark liquid and injected it into the sad-looking deer. .... (20) later the deer closed its eyes for the last time. .... (21) I felt the tears welling up in my eyes.

It (be) (22) a sad end to an otherwise beautiful day in the country. .... (23) I never liked driving down narrow country lanes with high hedges.

GUIDED WRITING

Composition task

Below are the first and last paragraphs of a description of what happened when a student took part in a parachute jump.

Imagine you are the student and complete the composition. Use the questions provided to help you.

COMPOSITION 4

INTRODUCTION

Paragraph 1 Three years ago I volunteered to take part in a sponsored parachute jump to raise money for the Cancer Research Campaign. It turned out to be the most exciting experience I have ever had.

THE DAY BEFORE

Paragraph 2 The preparation:
What training did you receive?

THE BIG DAY

Paragraph 3 Before the flight:
Who else was going to jump?
What did you do before you got on the plane?
What was the weather like?

Paragraph 4 The flight:
How many people were with you in the plane?
How were they trying to calm their nerves?
How did you feel?

Paragraph 5 The jump:
Were you one of the first to jump?
What happened when you jumped?
How did you feel?

Paragraph 6 The descent:
What happened?
Where did you come down?
Did you hurt yourself?

CONCLUSION

Paragraph 7 In the minibus on the way back to the parachute centre we all felt a great sense of relief that our ordeal was over. Some people said that they would love to do it again but, as for me, I felt sure that my first parachute jump would also be my last.

You should write about 150 words.

YOU CAN PARACHUTE
JUST FOR FUN
at
Ipswich Parachute Centre
• 1 hour from London
• 2-day beginners' courses from £52 inclusive (weekend or midweek)
• Age limits – 16-55
• You are welcome to try just one static line jump or become a regular and progress to free fall
For further information and colour brochure
Telephone Ipswich (0473) 76547
or return this slip to: Ipswich Parachute Centre, Ipswich Airport, Ipswich IP3 9QF
Name
Address
Post Code

4 Directed writing exercises (1)

PRESENTATION

In Section B of Paper 3, Use of English, you will be asked to do a directed writing exercise.
In the following exercises you are asked to select information from a text and reproduce it in a different form.

Study the following directed writing exercise.

DIRECTED WRITING EXERCISE 1

[1]

Julie and Stephen have saved up £3,000 in order to buy a car. Read the following conversation and then continue the four paragraphs below in about 50 words each.

Stephen Hey, guess what? I think I may have found just the right car for us.

Julie Really?

Stephen Yes. One of the guys at work has got a Volkswagen Golf that he wants to sell. It's only four years old and he is asking £2,750, which seems pretty cheap to me. They're very good cars, you know – solid, well-built, reliable – should last for years.

Julie Yes, the *Know Your Car* magazine did say they were very reliable, but also that they're not that cheap to run – they tend to use up a lot of petrol around town and spare parts are rather expensive. And anyway we'd agreed to buy a new car, not one that's already been driven around for four years.

Stephen Yes, you're right, but I think this is too good an opportunity to miss. Also, Volkswagens last for years, you know. Four years is nothing for a VW.

Julie Well, that depends on how well it's been looked after, doesn't it? I mean, it's always a risk buying a second-hand car, even from someone you know. You don't get a guarantee with it, do you? And it'd be rather embarrassing if something went seriously wrong with it just after you bought it from this chap.

Stephen Well, it's only done 20,000 miles, which isn't very much in four years, and it's been regularly serviced. John – that's the guy's name – says he'll bring in all the bills to show me.

Julie Well, that's something I suppose.

[2]

Stephen Yes, and it'd be the ideal size for you to learn to drive in, as well as being big enough to take all four of us in comfortably. Also it's a fairly powerful car – it's a 1600 cc model – so it'd be ideal for driving long distances in, like when we go to your parents in Manchester.

Julie Well, it may well be all those things you say, but it's still a second-hand car. And I think it could turn out to be uneconomical, especially if anything goes wrong with it. I don't know, I still think we should get a new car. Then we'd be absolutely sure it was in perfect condition. Also, it would come with a two-year warranty, so they'd repair it free of charge if anything went wrong. In fact, this friend of mine at work has just bought a brand new Citroën 2 CV for under £3,000. I think they're lovely cars – so stylish!

Stephen Do you? I can't say I do.

Julie Oh, yes, they are. And according to *Know Your Car* they're incredibly reliable because they're so simple that there are fewer things to go wrong. Also they do 56 miles to a gallon on long runs, which makes them the most economical small cars on the market. And they're convertible so you can fold the roof back in summer. Sounds perfect to me!

Stephen Mm, but if it's so simple then it means that it's very basic – in other words not very comfortable. I expect they're very cold in winter, for example. Also, they only do 70 miles per hour maximum speed, so it'd be a long, tiring journey up to Manchester on the motorway. Added to that, they've got no acceleration whatsoever, so it'd be impossible to overtake anything, oh, apart from a tractor, perhaps, but only if the wind was behind you! And the suspension's terrible on those things – you'd have a pretty sore behind after 200 miles on the motorway!

Julie I think the main reason you wouldn't want one is that you'd be worried about your image.

Stephen What do you mean?

Julie Well, most of your friends seem to drive fast, sporty, 'masculine'-type cars, don't they? I think you'd feel a bit embarrassed about turning up at the rugby club in a 2 CV!

Stephen Mm, you may have a point there!

[3]

1 Stephen thinks they should buy the Volkswagen Golf because ....
....

2 Julie, on the other hand, feels that it might not be such a good idea to buy a Volkswagen Golf because ....
....

3 Julie would rather buy a new 2 CV because ....
....

4 Stephen, however, is against buying a 2 CV because ....
....

Below are some notes which summarise the main points of Stephen's arguments in favour of the Volkswagen Golf and Julie's against it.

IN FAVOUR OF VW (Stephen)	AGAINST VW (Julie)
good buy; solid, well-built, reliable; low mileage; serviced regularly; ideal for Julie to learn to drive in; big enough for whole family; fast – good for long journeys	not very economical to run: uses lots of petrol and spare parts expensive; risky buying second hand – no guarantee; embarrassing if it breaks down

Notice that, where possible, the ideas have been expressed using different words from those underlined in the conversation. Your paragraphs should not contain too many direct quotations from the conversation.

The notes above could be developed so as to complete the first two paragraphs, as on the right:

1 *Stephen thinks they should buy the Volkswagen Golf because ... it would be a very good buy at £2,750, especially since Volkswagens have such a good reputation for being solid, well-built, reliable cars. In addition, John's car has a low mileage and has been serviced regularly. He also feels that it would be ideal for Julie to learn to drive in. Finally, he points out that it would be good for long journeys because it is both fast and big enough for the whole family to fit comfortably.*

2 *Julie, on the other hand, feels that it would not be such a good idea to buy a Volkswagen Golf because ... it would not be very economical to run, for two reasons: firstly, it would use a lot of petrol driving in town and, secondly, the spare parts would be expensive if it needed repairing. Besides, she thinks that it is risky buying a second-hand car as there is no guarantee. Her last point is that it would be rather embarrassing if the car broke down.*

ANALYSIS

Linking ideas

Notice the following stylistic features.

1 the use of connectors such as **since**, **and** and **because** to link the clauses
2 the use of connectors and connecting phrases such as **firstly**, **in addition** and **her last point is that** to list the points of the argument
3 the use of reporting verbs such as **think**, **feel** and **point out** to introduce Stephen and Julie's opinions

Useful language

CONNECTING CLAUSES

because, as/since
so, so/such ... that
(in order) to/so as to, so that
but, however, although/(even) though, whereas
if, unless, in case, provided that/on condition that
and, both ... and, also, as well as, or, either ... or, not only ... but also

REPORTING POINTS

He thinks/feels/finds/believes that ...
In her opinion/view, According to him ...
She adds/goes on to say that ...
He suggests ...
She points out that ...
He argues that ...
She (dis)agrees that ...

INTRODUCING POINTS

Firstly, Secondly, Finally/Lastly ...
In the first place/To begin with ...
Her first (second, next, last) point (reason) is that ...
Another point he makes is that ...
Another reason why she ...
Moreover/Furthermore, In addition/Besides/Also ...
Apart from this/that ...

PRACTICE

Exercise 1

1 *Read the conversation again and then, with a pencil, underline the main points of Julie's arguments in favour of the 2 CV and Stephen's against it. Put a tick (√) beside the arguments in favour and a cross (×) beside the arguments against.*

2 *Make notes summarising the main points of the two arguments, as in the example on page 27, using your own words where possible.*

IN FAVOUR OF 2 CV (Julie)	AGAINST 2 CV (Stephen)
....	....
....	....
....	....
....	....
....	....

3 *Develop your notes so as to complete Paragraph 3 and Paragraph 4 in about 50 words each.*

Exercise 2

Report the following people's opinions, introducing them with a suitable verb or phrase, such as those listed below, and using your own words where possible.

agree believe point out add go on to say suggest feel in (his) opinion

1 Helen Yes, Chris, you're right when you say that cigarettes should be banned in cinemas and theatres but . . .
e.g. **Helen agrees that people shouldn't be allowed to smoke in cinemas and theatres.**

2 Adam Well, I think that one of the best ways of improving the standard of teaching in our schools would be to inspect teachers regularly in the classroom.

3 Gerry Yes, and don't forget that the Royal Family act as ambassadors for the United Kingdom when they visit other countries.

4 Kate Another reason I don't want to go on a package holiday is that the people who go on them are usually rather unadventurous and boring.

5 David Yes, and besides the moral question, bringing back capital punishment wouldn't deter fanatical terrorists like the IRA from carrying out their attacks.

6 Mary If you ask me, the only realistic chance of bringing about change in South Africa is to use economic sanctions against the régime.

7 Trevor Why not make all town centres pedestrian-only areas? That would make them much pleasanter places to go to.

8 Janet I don't think people should be allowed to drink at all if they're driving – not even one drink!

Exercise 3

First read the following two paragraphs, which summarise the main points of two opposing arguments, and then fill in the gaps.
Use the sample paragraphs on page 27 and the lists of connectors and reporting verbs in ***Useful language*** *to help you. Try to use as many different words and phrases as possible.*

1 Martin .... his grandmother should go into the Green Pastures Retirement Home for several .... : in the first .... , she can no longer look after herself properly .... the family cannot afford to employ a full-time nurse. .... , he .... that his grandmother has always said that she did not wish to be a burden to anybody when she got older. .... reason why he .... that she would be happier in the home is that several of her friends are already living there. .... , although he realises that it would cost quite a lot of money, he .... that it would be worth the expense so that they could be sure that she was being well cared for.

2 Carol, on the other hand, ... that it is the family's duty to look after her grandmother, especially .... she's so ill. She .... that it would be wrong to send her to a home .... the old lady would feel as if she were just waiting to die .... that her family regarded her as a burden. She .... that people who are seriously ill need their family's love and affection and that they are much more likely to get better .... they feel wanted. .... , she .... that each one of them should give up some of their free time in order to take turns at looking after her.

Exercise 4

DIRECTED WRITING EXERCISE 2

In a television debate on the motion 'Britain should abandon its nuclear energy programme and close down all of its nuclear power stations' Angela Freeman, Chairperson of People for Ecology, argued for the motion and Sir Peter Adamson, Secretary of State for Energy, against.

1 *Read the following notes, which summarise the main points of the two arguments.*

FOR	AGAINST
1 element of risk – not impossible that Chernobyl-type accident will happen in UK 2 just one accident could expose thousands to radiation – cancer deaths? 3 radiation leaks – contamination (agriculture, cattle) 4 nuclear energy is a new technology – dangers not fully understood 5 waste radioactive for thousands of years – nowhere to store it safely 6 real reason for nuclear power stations – to produce plutonium for nuclear weapons	1 safety standards at power stations extremely high – chance of an accident like Chernobyl 1 in 10,000 years 2 most radiation leaks very small – no danger to population; result of serious accident – 30-40 deaths from cancer 3 safety record of nuclear industry very good – more workers die or are injured in accidents every year in coal industry or oil industry 4 great deal of research into nuclear energy and effects of radiation 5 nuclear energy cheaper than coal or oil 6 we will need nuclear energy to replace coal and oil when supplies end

2 *Develop the notes so as to complete the following two paragraphs in about 100 words each.*

Angela Freeman is very much in favour of the motion because

....

Sir Peter Adamson is totally against the motion because ....

....

GUIDED WRITING

Composition task

DIRECTED WRITING EXERCISE 3

Lee Evans spent a week on a canoeing holiday in Wales with a group of scouts.

Look at the newspaper cutting and the entries in his diary on page 32.

Imagine that you are Lee Evans. Complete the letter he wrote to his friend Anthony telling him about the trip.

Use the following technique to help you.

1 Read the letter and then underline any information in the newspaper cutting and diary which you think could be used to complete each section suitably.
2 Using your own words where possible, make notes summarising the most important information.
3 Using suitable connectors to link your clauses (**and**, **because**, **as** etc.) and sentences (**Then**, **Next**, **After that** etc.), develop your notes so as to complete each section of the letter.

SPARE A MINUTE FOR AFRICA
WORKOUT FOR SPORT AID

Thank you for sparing a minute for Africa and supporting this universally acclaimed cause by working out for Sport Aid. Please obtain as many sponsors as you can and raise as much money as possible, because every penny you raise in sponsorship will go directly to aid the starving people of Africa.
And remember, there is an African dying from starvation every ten minutes and it takes only £50 to keep an African alive for a whole year.

BOB GELDOF

BAND AID UNICEF

On May 25th we'd like you to take part in a workout for Sport Aid. You can do this by joining your local aerobic or keep fit group or, you can ...

HOW TO OBTAIN YOUR 'WORKOUT' FOR SPORT AID SPONSORSHIP FORM
To obtain your sponsorship form you will need to pay an entry fee of £2.00.
You will receive by return a sponsorship form

LOCAL SCOUTS RAISE £1,000 FOR AFRICA

Ten venture scouts from the 89th Maidenhead Scout Group have just returned home after a 100-mile sponsored canoe down the River Wye in Wales, which raised over £1,000 for Bob Geldof's Band Aid Trust charity.

The trip had originally been planned as part of The Duke of Edinburgh Award Scheme but after hearing about Sport Aid the scouts decided to kill two birds with one stone.

Lee Evans, 22, the group leader, explained:

'The idea that we could use our canoeing expedition to do something positive to help other people had never occurred to us. Then, a few weeks ago, we saw an advert for Sport Aid on TV encouraging people to raise money for the starving in Africa by taking part in sponsored sports events. So we decided that each one of us should try to get 25 people to pledge 5p a mile for every mile we canoed on the 7- day trip.'

The venture scouts had spent most of their spare time during the first six months of 1987 building the fibre-glass canoes in preparation for their week-long camping and canoeing expedition in Wales.

They set off from Rhayader last Monday, their canoes loaded with tents, sleeping-bags, spare clothes and 7 days' supplies of food. At the end of each day's canoeing they sought permission at the nearest farmhouse before pitching their tents in one of the farmer's fields and either cooking an open-air supper of sausages, eggs and bacon or walking to the nearest village for fish and chips. They eventually reached Ross-on-Wye yesterday afternoon, having canoed just over 100 miles, an average of 14 miles a day.

'It was a fantastic achievement for the lads,' enthused Lee Evans, 'They should feel proud that they've managed to combine a holiday with raising £1,000 for such a worthwhile cause. I hope other Maidenhead scouts will follow their fine example.'

4

MONDAY 4 SEPT

12.15 – left Rhayader. Perfect weather – not a cloud in the sky. Canoe seemed very heavy with all the luggage – tent, sleeping-bag, billy-cans, camping gaz – arms aching after ½ an hour. 3.00 – stopped for well-deserved picnic lunch – sandwiches – in field by the river. Lunch ended abruptly when we realised that cows coming towards us were in fact bulls! 4.00 – river too shallow – had to carry canoes 200 yards! 5.45 – DISASTER STRIKES – trying to get light for cigarette from Colin – lost balance and canoe rolled over – didn't panic – climbed out underwater and swam to the bank – BUT everything inside canoe including sleeping-bag wet through – YUK! 8.00 – stopped near farmhouse – farmer very friendly – gave us permission to camp in his field – ALSO he offered to dry my wet clothes, sleeping-bag etc. AND lent me blankets to sleep under. Bacon & eggs for dinner – then off to nearby pub to keep warm (and dry) and to play darts – slept very well!

SUNDAY 10 SEPT

5.00 – THE END of the "canoe-athon"! Reached Ross-on-Wye – minibuses waiting for us AND photographer from local paper! Everybody EXHAUSTED – we'd canoed 20 miles that day. What a RELIEF to finish! All my muscles ache – looking forward to getting back to a proper bed tonight. So tired I could sleep for a week!

Dear Anthony,

Sorry I wasn't here when you phoned last weekend but, as I'm sure my mother told you, ...

....

The idea of the expedition was to ....

....

By the end of the week we had ....
and ....

We took all our camping equipment with us in the canoes. Every night we ....

....

The canoeing itself was great fun, once you got used to the extra weight, but on the first day I had rather an unfortunate accident. ....

....

Luckily, the farmer, who had let us camp in his field, ...

....

On the last day ....

....

I was glad it was all over because ....

....

Anyway, now you know why I couldn't make it to your party on Saturday. Hope you had a great time.

See you soon,

Lee

5 Narratives (2)

ANALYSIS

Text organisation

The sentences in the composition below are in the wrong order.

1 *In pairs, put them in the correct order (1–15) and decide where the composition should be divided into paragraphs.*

COMPOSITION 1

a For the last few minutes he had been wondering what was behind the beautifully ornate door behind the large group of tourists. ☐

b The only light in it came from a single candle which was standing on an old wooden table in the centre of the room. ☐

c The next thing Philip knew he was falling through the air. ☐

d The castle guide was explaining how, in the fifteenth century, a princess had leapt to her death from the top of the watch tower. ☐

e All of a sudden, the door slammed shut behind him and Philip heard the key being turned in the lock. ☐

f Then Philip noticed that there was another door in the darkest corner of the room. ☐

g Suddenly, the candle flame flickered as if in a draught and Philip felt the hairs on the back of his neck stand up. ☐

h Fortunately, they all had their backs to him so nobody saw Philip silently open it and slip into the room beyond. ☐

i He banged on the door with his fist and shouted, 'Let me out!' as loud as he could but, to his astonishment, nobody heard him. ☐

j Luckily, it was not locked and when he turned the handle it flew open in front of him. ☐

k Philip, however, was no longer paying any attention to what she was saying. ☐

l He found himself in a dark, windowless room which seemed so inhospitable that he immediately felt a shiver run down his spine. ☐

m To his horror, he realised that it had almost reached the end of its wick and that the room would shortly be plunged into total darkness. ☐

n Seconds later he opened his eyes and was very relieved to find himself lying on the floor beside his bed. ☐

o Then, suddenly, he felt an immensely strong pair of hands lift him up and throw him violently through the door. ☐

2 *When you have finished, look at the pronouns in each sentence and indicate which words they refer back to.*

e.g. f Then **Philip** noticed that there was another **door** in the darkest corner of the room.

j Luckily, **it** was not locked and when **he** turned the handle **it** flew open in front of **him** .

PRACTICE

Exercise 1

Fill in the gaps in the following paragraphs with suitable pronouns.

1 Fortunately, Santos was not seriously injured when .... lost control of .... car and crashed in the final stages of the Belgian Grand Prix. .... was leading at the time and if .... had won .... he would certainly have won the 1987 Formula 1 drivers' world championship.

2 Richard and I were delighted with the room that .... were given. .... was clean, modern, comfortable and .... had .... own fully equipped bathroom. But what .... liked most about .... was that .... had a balcony which overlooked the sea.

3 Mary had not mentioned to .... parents that .... new boyfriend was nearly twenty years older than .... So imagine .... surprise when .... met .... for the first time. After all, ... was only a couple of years younger than ....

PRESENTATION

Read the following composition, in which the writer describes what happened when he went to watch a royal wedding procession.

COMPOSITION 2

Although there were two or three people in front of us I had a marvellous view because I was sitting on my father's shoulders. It was now half past twelve and we had arrived very early that morning, at eight, so that we could get a good position from which to watch the royal wedding procession.

We had listened to the ceremony on our transistor radio and had heard that the procession would be passing us at any minute now on its way to Buckingham Palace. We knew it could not be far away now as we could hear people cheering further down the road. I felt very excited.

Then I heard somebody shout, 'Here they come!' and, all of a sudden, the people behind us started pushing forward, in the hope of getting a better view. I began to feel very unsafe up there on my father's shoulders. However, we were so tightly packed together by now that I could not have got down even if I had wanted to.

Now I could see the first carriage approaching. In it I could just make out the smiling faces of the prince and his bride. Then, suddenly, just as the horse-drawn carriage drew level with us, I saw a woman in front of us leap over the barrier. To my surprise, the policeman standing just to the right of us was looking the other way and the woman started running across the road towards the prince's carriage.

By this time the policeman had noticed what had happened and was chasing after her as fast as he could. When she got to the royal carriage the woman pulled out a gun and raised it towards the prince.

Everything seemed to be happening in slow motion, as it sometimes does in nightmares. The policeman threw himself at the woman and, a split second later, we heard the gun go off and saw the royal couple dive to the floor of their carriage. The crowd around us had stopped cheering. They seemed to be holding their breath as they waited for the outcome of this drama.

Ten seconds later, to everyone's relief, the prince and his bride emerged from the bottom of the carriage, badly shaken but otherwise unhurt. A huge cheer went up all around us.

Luckily, the policeman had managed to deflect the attacker's aim and the bullet had missed its target by inches. By this time the would-be assassin was being led away by half a dozen policemen. Meanwhile, the procession continued on its way as if nothing out of the ordinary had happened.

5

ANALYSIS

Linking ideas

First find the sentences in Composition 2 that mean the same as the following sentences and then fill in the gaps choosing suitable connectors from the list below.

1 The writer was not at the front of the crowd .... he was sitting on his father's shoulders .... he could see everything perfectly.
2 They had got there early .... they wanted to find a good place from where to view the procession.
3 They could hear the cheers of the crowd further down the street .... they knew the procession was approaching.
4 .... he did not feel very safe on his father's shoulders, he could not have got down .... everybody was so squashed together.
5 At first the policeman did not notice that the woman had jumped over the barrier .... he was facing in the opposite direction.
6 .... he realised what she was going to do he ran after her at full speed.
7 .... the prince and his bride saw the attacker they dived for cover.
8 .... the royal couple were suffering from shock they were not injured.

---

and   but   so   as   because   although   since   as soon as   when   so that   however

Useful language

When writing a narrative it is a good idea to tell the reader about the feelings or emotions experienced by the people involved.

Find examples of this in Composition 1 and Composition 2 and then complete the following tables.

Table 1

NOUN		
To	my	surprise
	our	....
	his/her	....
	their	....

Table 2

PAST PARTICIPLE			
I		surprised	
we	was	astonished	when . . .
he/she	were	horrified	to . . .
they		....	

Table 3

ADJECTIVE/PAST PARTICIPLE		
I we he/she they	felt	afraid exhausted ....

PRACTICE

Exercise 2

Re-write the sentences below to emphasise the feelings or emotions experienced by the people in each case.
Use the constructions shown in Table 1 and Table 2 and choose from the following words.

amazement (n.)	relief (n.)	delight (n.)	disappointment (n.)	horror (n.)	amusement (n.)
amazed (p.p.)	relieved (p.p.)	delighted (p.p.)	disappointed (p.p.)	horrified (p.p.)	amused (p.p.)

e.g. We all laughed when the clown threw a custard pie in my father's face.

To our amusement, } the clown threw a custard pie in my father's face.
We were all amused when }

1 When Carol found out that her husband was not on the hijacked aeroplane she felt much better.
2 Believe it or not, the clock struck thirteen times!
3 When Jane returned to the car park she found that her car had been stolen.
4 Matthew had been hoping to pass his driving test first time but he failed.
5 When she learned that she had won first prize she was happy.

Exercise 3

Complete the following sentences using the construction shown in Table 3.

e.g. Before the exam I ....
Before the exam I **felt very nervous/apprehensive/worried.**

1 When I heard the news that John Lennon had been assassinated I ....
....

2 After watching the late-night horror film on TV by myself I ....

3 After three hours alone in the broken lift she ....

4 We had won our previous ten matches so when we arrived at the stadium we ....
....

5 As we had not slept for thirty-six hours I ....

5

ANALYSIS

Gerund or infinitive?

1 *Fill in the gaps in the following sentences from Composition 1 and Composition 2.*

a ... nobody saw Philip silently .... it and .... into the room beyond.

b ... he felt an immensely strong pair of hands .... him up and .... him violently through the door.

c ... we could hear people .... further down the road.

d Then I heard somebody .... , 'Here they come!'

e Now I could see the first carriage ....

f ... we heard the gun .... and saw the royal couple .... to the floor of their carriage.

2 *In pairs, discuss the difference in meaning between the following sentences.*

I heard somebody **shout**, 'Help!'.
I heard somebody **shouting**, 'Help!'.

3 *Now read sentence* **i** *in Composition 1 again and complete the following sentence.*

Nobody heard Philip .... and ....

see, **feel**, **hear** and **watch** are often used in these constructions.
Which other verbs could also be used in this way?

PRACTICE

Exercise 4

Fill in the gaps in the following sentences.

1 I knew it must be almost dawn because I could .... all the birds .... in the garden.

2 We .... the two cars .... into each other but did not see how the accident happened as we were behind a bus at the time.

3 They .... the children .... their sandcastles for a few minutes and then continued their walk along the beach.

4 When James .... Alison .... at the bus-stop he stopped to offer her a lift.

Exercise 5

First read the composition below and then fill in the gaps and write a suitable last paragraph.
Use Composition 1 and Composition 2 to help you.

COMPOSITION 3

At seven o'clock I got into my car, a brand new Alfa Romeo, and turned the key. To .... , ... would not start. Then I noticed that the needle in the fuel gauge was not moving and realised that I had run out of petrol. It was obviously not my lucky day.

I had arranged to meet Caroline outside the ABC cinema in the High Street at seven-thirty. I was determined not to be late, especially .... this was to be our first date.

So I decided to leave my car and catch the bus into town instead. However, I was only a hundred yards from the bus-stop when, ... , I saw my bus .... the corner and .... the bus-stop. I ran towards .... as .... could but, ... as I reached the stop, ... set off. I banged on the door to attract the driver's attention. .... turned round and smiled .... I thought he was going to stop and let me on. .... , to .... , he accelerated and drove off without me. I felt so .... I could have strangled .... !

The next .... was not for another half an hour .... I set off on foot, half walking, half running. Three quarters of an hour .... , I arrived at the beginning of the High Street.

By .... it was eight o'clock and the film would have already begun. I was so .... by now .... I thought Caroline would have given up waiting and gone home. .... , as I got nearer the cinema I could .... on the pavement. .... seemed to be waving at someone. Then, ... , a taxi pulled up outside the cinema. I shouted 'Caroline, wait!' as .... I could but .... could not hear me above the noise of the traffic. I sprinted the final fifty yards to the cinema ....
....

....

....

....

GUIDED WRITING

Composition task

Below is the first paragraph of an eye-witness's account of a serious road accident.

Imagine that you are the eye-witness and complete the account. Use the questions provided to help you and write between 120 and 180 words.

COMPOSITION 4

INTRODUCTION

Paragraph 1 One December evening two years ago I was walking home from work when I witnessed a terrible road accident between .... I remember that it was an extremely cold, windy night and that it had just started raining.

THE ACCIDENT

Paragraph 2 Where were you? What did you hear? What did you see?

IMMEDIATELY AFTERWARDS

Paragraph 3 What had happened? Was anybody hurt? What did you do? What did the other people present do? How did you feel?

A LITTLE LATER

Paragraph 4 When did the police and ambulance(s) arrive? How had they found out about it? What did they do? What did you do? What happened next?

SOME TIME LATER

Paragraph 5 What did you tell the police? Did you have to appear in court? What happened to the people involved in the accident?

CONCLUSION

Paragraph 6 Whose fault was the accident? Why?

6 Formal letters

El Rossinyol Apartments
ACCOMMODATION
• can sleep up to 5
• spacious living area
• open-plan kitchen
• luxury shower-room
• private terrace
LOCATION AND FACILITIES
• 10 minutes' walk to fine, sandy beach
• large swimming pool
• 6 tennis courts
• bar, snack bar and TV room
• babysitting service available
maid service: every day
welcome grocery pack on arrival
Sun Kist

PRESENTATION

Read the following letter, in which James complains to the company which arranged his family's holiday in Majorca.

LETTER 1

15, Avon Street
Warwick
CV34 8RA

The Manager
Sunkist Holidays
327 Oxford Street
London W1 3SA

15th September 1987

Dear Sir/Madam

I am writing to complain about a two-week holiday at "El Rossinyol" apartments in Majorca, which my family and I booked through your company. The holiday number was A 1773 and the dates were 13th - 27th August.

Firstly, there was no representative of your company to meet us at the airport. We learned later that the mini-bus had broken down earlier in the day. Moreover, the taxi drivers were on strike so we had to walk half a mile to the nearest bus-stop, where we waited almost two hours for a bus. Eventually, after a thirty-minute walk at the other end, we arrived at the apartments at one o'clock in the morning.

Secondly, none of the apartments had been cleaned since the previous occupants had left. Fortunately, we found some clean sheets in one of the cupboards. When we complained to the courier about this she told us that the cleaning lady had been ill for several days.

Thirdly, your brochure stated that "El Rossinyol" was 'a pleasant, ten-minute stroll from a fine, sandy beach'. However, we found that it was over half an hour's walk along an extremely busy main road and that the beach was pebbly, overcrowded and rather dirty.

Finally, whereas the brochure said that 'evenings are fairly quiet at "El Rossinyol"', there was, in fact, an incredibly noisy disco opposite the apartments. This made it impossible to go to bed before three o'clock in the morning.

To sum up, this was the worst holiday my family and I have ever been on. The standard of service was appalling and your brochure gave a misleading description of the facilities. Therefore, I feel that we are entitled to a full refund of the cost of the holiday.

I hope this matter will receive your prompt attention.

Yours faithfully

James Harper

6

ANALYSIS

Linking ideas

Using the underlined words to help you, complete the following sentences about Letter 1.

1 James is writing this letter in order to ....

2 He gives .... reasons why he didn't enjoy the holiday.

3 The Harpers had to get the bus from the airport because ....

and ....

4 The brochure said the apartments were ten minutes' walk from the beach but ....

....

5 The Harpers couldn't go to bed before three o'clock in the morning because ....

....

Text organisation

The sentences in the following letter are in the wrong order.

In pairs, put them in the correct order (1–10) and decide where the letter should be divided into paragraphs.

SUMMER JOBS ABROAD

Energetic, practically-minded young people required to work in 1987 on European camp-sites as representatives for the UK's leading camping and caravanning company. Full or half season. Some positions also available for senior representatives and drivers/warehouse assistants.
Applications from couples, or from candidates available from March/April particularly welcome
Knowledge of one major European language usually required.
For application form please write to: Catherine Atkinson, Couriers Dept, Eurocamp Travel Limited, Tatton Street, Knutsford, Cheshire WA16 6BG.

Eurocamp

LETTER 2

18, Cedar Close
Bath
BA2 6DO
6th April 1987

Catherine Atkinson
Couriers Dept.
Eurocamp Travel Limited
Tatton Street
Knutsford WA16 6BG

Dear Ms. Atkinson,

a Besides having a sound academic knowledge of these languages, I worked for three months as an au-pair in Grenoble when I left school. ☐

b With regard to my availability for work, my first year exams will have finished by the end of June. ☐

c Finally, as I will be in Manchester for the week 27th April - 1st May it would be convenient for me to attend an interview during this time. ☐

d As regards my ability to speak Italian, I have had an Italian pen-friend since I was fourteen and have spent two summers with her and her family in Milan. ☐

e I saw your advertisement in today's Guardian newspaper and would like to apply for a job as a representative in Europe this summer. ☐

f I look forward to hearing from you. ☐

g I am currently taking the first year of a European Studies degree course at Bath University. ☐

h Therefore, I would be free to work for your organisation from the beginning of July until mid September, as required. ☐

i As you will see from my curriculum vitae (enclosed), I obtained good 'A' level grades in both French and Italian. ☐

j This course includes French language and literature as well as Italian conversation classes so I am keeping up my languages. ☐

Yours sincerely

Tricia Adamson

TRICIA ADAMSON

Register

1 As Tricia does not know the person she is writing to she has used formal language in her letter.

Find the examples of formal language in Letter 2 which have more or less the same meaning as the following more informal phrases.

INFORMAL	FORMAL
I want to apply	**I would like to apply**
As for when I can start work	....
I could come for an interview	....
As for my Italian	....
Write soon	....
So I could work	....
as you like	....
It says on my c.v.	....
I got good A levels	....

2 *In pairs, discuss the differences between the two formal letters written by James and Tricia in this unit and the two informal letters written by Dave and Tina in Unit 1.*

Consider the following:

the sender's address
the recipient's address
the salutation (**Dear ...**)
words used to begin paragraphs
contractions (e.g. **haven't**)
the purpose of the first paragraph (e.g. to apologise for not writing sooner)
the purpose of the final paragraph (e.g. to explain why he must finish the letter now)
closing remarks (e.g. **Hope to see you in two weeks' time.**)
signing off (e.g. **Yours**)

3 When should the following salutations be used?

Dear Sir Dear Madam Dear Sir/Madam Dear Mr ...
Dear Mrs ... Dear Ms ... Yours faithfully
Yours sincerely

Useful language

TYPICAL FIRST SENTENCES	TYPICAL LAST SENTENCES
I am writing to { ask/enquire (about) ... / request ... / confirm (that) ... / apologise for ... / complain (about) ... } I am writing in { reply/response to ... / connection with ... } I would like to { apply for ... / express my concern ... } With reference to your (letter) ... I saw your (advertisement) ... Thank you for your letter of (5th July) ...	I look forward to { hearing from you. / meeting you. } Thank you again for your kind cooperation. Thanking you in advance for your assistance/ cooperation in this matter. I hope that this matter will receive your prompt attention.

PRACTICE

Exercise 1

In pairs, decide when you would use each of the first and last sentences above.
Think of an example for each of the first sentences.

e.g. I am writing in reply to **your advertisement for the post of editor which appeared in *The Times* on 6th January**.

Exercise 2

Write a first sentence and a last sentence for each of the following:

1 a letter to a hotel – you think you may have lost your wedding ring there
2 a letter to your bank – you think there is a mistake in your statement
3 a letter to a holiday company – you would like to see some of their brochures
4 a letter to a hotel – you did not enjoy your stay there for a number of reasons

5 a letter to a business associate – you were unable to arrive at a meeting because your train was delayed
6 a letter to a travel agent's – you ordered some airline tickets six weeks ago and you still have not received them

Exercise 3

In pairs, look at the following sentences from Letter 1 and Letter 2. Decide which of the four connecting words or phrases below could be used instead of the ***highlighted*** *word to express the same idea as in the original sentence.*

In some cases it will be necessary to put the connecting word or phrase in a different position in the sentence. In other cases it will be necessary to make two sentences where previously there was only one or to join two sentences together.

e.g. Finally, as I expect to be in Manchester for the week 27th April–1st May it would be convenient for me to attend an interview during this time. (Letter 2, c)

A therefore B so C for this reason D furthermore

1 Firstly, there was no representative of your company to meet us at the airport. **Moreover**, the taxi drivers were on strike so we had to walk half a mile to the nearest bus-stop ... (Letter 1, Paragraph 2)

A in addition B besides C what is more D on the other hand

2 Thirdly, your brochure stated that 'El Rossinyol' was 'a pleasant, ten-minute stroll from a fine, sandy beach'. **However**, we found that it was over half an hour's walk ... (Letter 1, Paragraph 4)

A although B therefore C whereas D but

3 Finally, **whereas** the brochure said that 'evenings are fairly quiet at "El Rossinyol"' there was, in fact, an incredibly noisy disco opposite the apartments. (Letter 1, Paragraph 5)

A however B although C while D in spite of the fact that

4 The standard of service was appalling and your brochure gave a misleading description of the facilities. **Therefore**, I feel that we are entitled to a full refund of the cost of the holiday. (Letter 1, Paragraph 6)

A for this reason B for this C consequently D furthermore

5 **Besides** having a sound academic knowledge of these languages, I worked for three months as an au-pair in Grenoble when I left school. (Letter 2, a)

A as well as B despite C as D in addition to

6 ... my first year exams will have finished by the end of June. **Therefore**, I would be free to work for your organisation from the beginning of July ... (Letter 2, b and h)

A however B as C consequently D since

Exercise 4

Look at the advertisement on the right and read the incomplete letter below.

LETTER 3

7. Mayes Road
Birmingham
B24 5TR

18th February 1987

....
....
....

Dear ....

...., asking for sponsors to support ActionAid's work in the Third World.

I teach in a primary school in Birmingham .... has children from a variety of ethnic groups .... am planning to involve my class in a project on a country in the developing world. .... most of the children in this class are of Asian origin, I thought it would be a good idea to base this project on India, Bangladesh or Nepal.

I understand from a friend of mine, ... teaches in London and is already a supporter of ActionAid, that it is possible to sponsor an individual child, a school or a specific community project such as providing a well or a goat.

................., I would be grateful if you could send me an information pack with details of your current projects in the above-mentioned countries. .... I would like some information about any available videos or films .... show the work ActionAid are engaged in. .... I would be interested in arranging a visit to the class by one of your Education Officers.

....
....

Sarah Spencer

THERE ARE MILLIONS
OF CHILDREN
IN URGENT NEED
OVERSEAS

Mr and Mrs Reynolds of The Wirral are sponsors to 14 year old Kavata Wambu (above) from East Africa.
Read inside how their regular suppo helping to transform life for Kavata, her famil and her entire community.

NOW YOU CAN HEL
ONE OF THEM TODA

For more information contact:
ActionAid, Hamlyn House, Archway,
London N19 5PG
Tel: 01-281 4101

*When you have obtained a clear idea of the purpose of the letter fill in the gaps. Use Letter 1 and Letter 2 as well as the sentences in **Useful language** on page 44 to help you.*

Exercise 5

1 *Read the letter on the right, in which a language school informs a student of the accommodation arrangements it has made for his stay in England.*

2 Below is the letter Jaime wrote to Mr Brown.

In pairs, re-write the letter, omitting any irrelevant information and making any corrections or improvements which you feel are necessary.

LETTER 4

Calle de las Flores, 7
Alicante, Spain

15/8/87

Mr Brown,

Hello, my name is Jaime Pujol. I'm going to study at the Shakespeare School of English for six weeks. The course is from 28th September until 7th November. Mrs Clarke (she's the Accommodation Officer) wrote me a letter last week and told me that she'd booked me a room in your house for six weeks. That's fine by me. Is it OK for you? I'll get to Birmingham International Airport at 16.45. My flight is Aviaco AO 1032 from Alicante to Birmingham. The travel agent who sold me the airline ticket told me that I should get a train from the airport to Birmingham New Street Station and then take a train at 18.10 from Moor Street Station to Stratford. He said it would arrive in Stratford at 19.09. Can you meet me at the station? If you can't, please send a map. I want to know how to get to your house from the station. Which bus should I take? Or perhaps it would be better to take a taxi? I'd like breakfast at eight o'clock. My first lesson is at half past nine so this should give me enough time to get to school. We normally have dinner at ten o'clock in Spain but I suppose I'll have to get used to eating earlier. I'll be at school all day so I don't want to have lunch at your house. For breakfast I like coffee, bread, butter and jam - not bacon and eggs! For dinner I don't mind what I eat, but I should warn you that I have a big appetite! See you in September.

Yours Jaime

SHAKESPEARE SCHOOL OF ENGLISH
Kenilworth Road, Stratford-upon-Avon, CV31 5RS

Sr Jaime Pujol
C/de las Flores,7
Alicante
Spain

Dear Sr Pujol

Thank you for your letter of 25th July.

I confirm your enrolment on our six-week intensive Business English course which begins on Monday, 28th September. I would be grateful if you could send me the registration fee of £50 by the end of August.

As requested, I have arranged your accommodation with an English family and have reserved a room for you from your arrival on 27th September until 7th November. The rent will be £60 a week and will include bed, breakfast, and an evening meal.

Landlord: Mr A Brown
Accommodation: 22, Woodland Rise
Stratford-upon-Avon,
CV37 5XT
England

Please write to the landlord confirming your reservation of a room in his house and informing him of your expected time of arrival and your meal requirements.

I look forward to meeting you in September.

Yours sincerely

Joyce Clarke

Joyce Clarke
Accommodation Officer

6

GUIDED WRITING

Essay planning

In pairs, make a plan for each of the following three letters.

1 a letter to the manager of an expensive restaurant – you ate there last night with some friends and were extremely disappointed by the food, the wine, the service, the noise etc. (*Compare Letter 1*)
2 a letter to a night club – you saw their advertisement in a music magazine for a disc jockey (*Compare Letter 2*)
3 a letter to an adventure holiday club – you saw their advertisement on TV and you'd like to know more about their rock climbing weeks in Scotland

Make notes for each of the following:

salutation Dear ....

Paragraph 1 ....

....

Paragraph 2 ....

....

Paragraph 3 ....

....

Paragraph 4 ....

....

Paragraph 5 ....

....

signature Yours ....

Composition task

LETTER 5

When you have finished, expand your notes for one of the letter topics above and write a letter of between 120 and 180 words.

7 Discursive essays (2)

PRESENTATION

Read the following essay about whether couples should live together before they get married.

ESSAY 1

> It is a good idea for young people to live together before getting married. Do you agree?

Twenty years ago, when my parents were in their early twenties, it was quite rare for young couples to live together before they got married. Nowadays, however, living together first is very common and in general I think that this is a very good thing, for the following reasons.

To begin with, if a couple live together first, they have to spend much more time with each other than when they are going out together. Therefore, living together gives them the chance to find out what their partner is really like as well as whether they get on well with each other when they are together so much.

Another reason for living together first is that it gives people the opportunity to discover their partner's attitude towards things like cooking, washing up and cleaning. Will they share these chores or will one partner be expected to do more than the other?

Finally, it is usually much more difficult for a husband and wife to get divorced than it is for an unmarried couple to split up. Getting divorced is never easy because there are nearly always bitter arguments over who keeps the house, the furniture, the car and, most importantly, the children. On the other hand, it is relatively simple for an unmarried couple to split up since they usually remain financially independent and do not have children.

In conclusion, I am in favour of living together first because it gives a couple a good idea of what it would be like to be married to their partner before they promise to spend the rest of their lives together.

7

ANALYSIS

Text organisation

There are five paragraphs in Essay 1.

1 *Look at the essay again and, in pairs, consider the following questions.*

a What is the purpose of the first paragraph?
b In which paragraph does the writer first tell us his/her opinion of living together before marriage?
c How many reasons does the writer give to support his/her point of view? In which paragraphs are the reasons given?
d What is the purpose of the final paragraph?

2 *Complete the table below, which shows the organisation of paragraphs 2, 3 and 4.*

Living together before marriage	
Points	Word or phrase which introduces each point
1	....
2 couple can find out if they agree about who should cook, wash up etc.	....
3	Finally

Linking ideas

Using the underlined words to help you, complete the following sentences about Essay 1.

1 It was unusual for unmarried couples to live together in the 1960s but these days it ....
....

2 If a couple live together first, they can discover whether they really have a good relationship with their partner because ....
....

3 When a marriage breaks up there are usually arguments about who should have the house, the furniture and the car and also about who should look after the children. Consequently, ...
....
....

4 Unmarried couples do not usually share all their money or have children. As a result, ...
....

5 Living together gives a couple the chance to find out what marriage would be like before they promise to stay together for the rest of their lives. Therefore, the writer ....
....
....

PRACTICE

Exercise 1

First, expand the notes on the next page to make two sentences.
Then link them together, using the following connectors.

consequently as because therefore so however
as a result since on the other hand although

e.g. a last 5 years – serious accidents – nuclear power stations
b now – lot of people – close down – all nuclear power stations

In the last five years there have been several serious accidents at nuclear power stations. **Consequently**, a lot of people now think that they should all be closed down.

or A lot of people now feel that all nuclear power stations ought to be closed down **because** there have been a number of serious accidents during the last five years.

1 a nowadays – lot of mothers – young children – carry on working
b my opinion – government – provide more crèches and nursery schools
2 a last two years – more police on duty – football matches
b now – less fighting – rival supporters – football stadiums
3 a scientists – many alternative energy sources – solar power, wind power
b no longer necessary – build nuclear power stations – this country
4 a always – terrible shortages – food – Africa
b every year – hundreds of thousands – Africans – die – hunger
5 a 30 years ago – nearly all children – single-sex schools
b these days – majority of schools – this country – mixed
6 a last season – less trouble – rival football fans – **inside** stadiums
b last season – fighting – rival fans – **outside** stadiums – increased
7 a France – electricity – cheaper – other European countries
b France – nuclear energy – produce – 65% – its electricity
8 a these days – many women – decide – have careers
b very common – couples – employ nannies – look after – babies

GUIDED WRITING

Essay planning

First consider the following statements and decide whether or not you agree with them. Then note down three points supporting your opinion in each case.

> **1** Military service is a complete waste of time and ought to be abolished.
> What do you think?

REASONS

1 ....

....

2 ....

....

3 ....

....

2 It is wrong to spend billions of dollars on space research when hundreds of thousands of people on Earth are suffering from malnutrition or dying of starvation. How far do you agree?

REASONS

1 ....

....

2 ....

....

3 ....

....

3 Blood sports such as fox hunting, bullfighting and cock fighting are barbaric and should therefore be banned. Do you agree?

REASONS

1 ....

....

2 ....

....

3 ....

....

Composition task

Choose one of the essay topics above and write an essay of between 120 and 180 words, using the structure suggested below.

First look again at the words and phrases in ***Useful language*** *on page 16.*

ESSAY 2

Paragraph 1	Introduce the subject of the essay and state why it is an important issue at the present time. Give your opinion on this issue.
Paragraph 2	Give the first point supporting your opinion.
Paragraph 3	Give the second point supporting your opinion.
Paragraph 4	Give the last point supporting your opinion.
Paragraph 5	Conclude the essay by summarising your opinion.

7

ANALYSIS

Text organisation

The sentences in the essay below are in the wrong order.

In pairs, put them in the correct order (1–9) and decide where the essay should be divided into paragraphs.

ESSAY 3

Too much importance is attached to exams at school. Do you agree?

a This is because one is much better at taking exams than the other. ☐

b However, like many other people, I feel that too much importance is given to exams and that it is time to change the way we monitor our children's development at school. ☐

c As a result, students are often encouraged to learn facts by heart, instead of how to use the information and how to think for themselves. ☐

d The traditional method of assessing academic progress has always been for students to take exams. ☐

e Apart from this, exam questions often test how much a student has remembered about the things he or she has been taught in the classroom. ☐

f To sum up, in my opinion less importance should be given to exams because they are unfair, because they are often a test of memory and because they can have a negative influence on teaching. ☐

g Lastly, it seems to me that exams sometimes have a bad effect on teaching, as teachers are usually judged by the exam results of their students. ☐

h Firstly, I think that the examination system is unfair because sometimes two students with the same ability in a subject get very different exam results. ☐

i Consequently, they are often more interested in preparing their students for the exams than in making their lessons lively and stimulating. ☐

GUIDED WRITING

Composition task

It is wrong to keep animals in captivity. Do you agree?

On the next page are a plan and some detailed notes for this essay.

Using the plan to help you, develop the notes into an essay of between 120 and 180 words. You need not include every point but should make sure that you develop your argument logically. Look again at the way you developed the notes using connectors in ***Exercise 1*** *on page 51.*

ESSAY 4

INTRODUCTION

Paragraph 1 many years – conservationists and animal rights groups – arguing that – wrong to keep animals in captivity – I disagree – following reasons:

REASON ONE – Saving from extinction

Paragraph 2 Many species of animal – in danger – extinction – their natural habitat – disappearing fast – spread of civilisation – if animals kept in captivity – can breed in safety – save species from dying out – e.g. certain eagles, giant pandas

REASON TWO – Better conditions

Paragraph 3 These days – many animals not in zoos – instead in safari parks – much more freedom, space than traditional zoos – animals no longer in tiny cages – better quality of life

REASON THREE – Education

Paragraph 4 If no animals in captivity – most people – never see exotic animals in real life – zoologists – not able to study animals – zoos, safari parks provide education and opportunity for scientific study and research

CONCLUSION

Paragraph 5 Many people think – animals in captivity = cruel, barbaric – I do not agree – zoologists – save from extinction – animals in captivity – better conditions – people can learn about animals – important research

8 Descriptions

PRESENTATION

Read the passage below, in which Michael describes the first morning of a holiday he spent in Venice.

COMPOSITION 1 (Part 1)

We got married in mid-November and went to Venice for our honeymoon. All of the people we knew who had been there had assured us that it would be an enchanting place to visit out of season, and they were right. I can honestly say that it is the most romantic city I have ever been to.

Although the wintry sun was shining brightly on the first morning of our stay in Venice we had an extremely cold, wet start to our holiday. We were just about to set out from our hotel to explore the city when we discovered, to our astonishment, that the street outside the front door was under a foot of water. The sea level had risen several feet during the night causing the canal by the hotel to overflow.

We certainly had no intention of staying in the hotel until the tide went out so we took off our shoes and socks, rolled up our trousers and waded through the freezing water. After about a hundred yards we got to a little square that had remained above the water level. When we finally emerged from the icy water our feet were blue with cold and we were shivering, so we made for the nearest cafe where we had a delicious cappuccino to warm us up.

After restoring the circulation to our feet we took the vaporetto (water bus) all the way down the Grand Canal to St Mark's Square. It must surely be one of the most beautiful bus journeys in the world. As the vaporetto winds its way down the Grand Canal you pass the exquisite facades of Gothic and Renaissance palaces, magnificent churches, the elegant Rialto Bridge and, of course, lots of little gondolas ferrying their passengers from one side of the canal to the other.

At St Mark's we discovered that the famous square was also under several inches of water but that Venetians and tourists alike were managing to keep their feet dry by walking on the raised duckboards, which the authorities had thoughtfully provided in case of such floods.

ANALYSIS

Text organisation

There are five paragraphs in the first part of Michael's description of his visit to Venice.
Complete the following summary of each paragraph.

Paragraph 1 First, Michael tells us that he .... in November and, on the recommendation of his friends .... for his honeymoon.

Paragraph 2 Then he describes what they found when ....

Paragraph 3 Next he explains how they .... and what they did as soon as they ....

Paragraph 4 After that he tells us that they .... and describes ....

Paragraph 5 Then he describes the scene at ....

Why does Michael begin a new paragraph in each case?

Ordering events

In pairs, put the following events from Composition 1 in the correct order (1–15), using the underlined *words to help you.*

a They found that the street was flooded. ☐
b They went to the café. ☐
c They got married. ☐
d They got on the *vaporetto.* ☐
e They took off their shoes and socks. ☐
f They reached the little square. ☐
g They went to Venice. ☐
h They arrived in St Mark's Square. ☐
i Friends advised them to go to Venice. ☐
j The town council put duckboards in St Mark's Square. ☐
k They walked through the water. ☐
l They felt better. ☐
m They started to shiver. ☐
n The canal overflowed. ☐
o The water level rose. ☐

8

PRACTICE

Exercise 1

First find an example in Composition 1 of each of the following constructions and then, using your imagination, complete the sentences.

1 I arrived at Charles De Gaulle Airport at just after seven o'clock **and** ....

2 **When** we **got** to our hotel we were furious to discover that the holiday company **had** ....

3 James **was just about to** set off for the station **when** ....

4 The lorry in front suddenly **screeched** to a halt **causing** .... **to** ....

5 **When** they eventually **found** Patricia she **was** ....

6 **After** .... she finally **got back** to the hotel at three o'clock in the morning.

ANALYSIS

Complete the following sentences from Composition 1.

I can honestly say that it is the ....
It must surely be ....

PRACTICE

Exercise 2

Make similar statements about each of the following:

a city a carnival a rock concert a tropical island a boat journey a hotel a night club
a sporting event a film a meal a person a building a day a holiday

e.g. New York is without doubt the most dangerous city I have ever visited.
I think New York is probably one of the most exciting cities in the world.

PRESENTATION

Read the second part of Michael's description of his visit to Venice.

COMPOSITION 1 (Part 2)

We began our sightseeing in the basilica. There we were particularly impressed by the beautiful, gold-painted mosaics on the walls and ceilings and by the magnificent palla d'oro, a solid gold altar-piece containing religious portraits and studded with precious gems.

However, the highlight of our visit to the basilica was the view from the balcony which overlooked St Mark's Square. By now it was almost midday and the water covering most of the streets and squares down below us glistened and sparkled in the brilliant sunlight. This gave the city a magical, unreal quality. It was as if Venice were floating out to sea. The view from the balcony was so lovely that we stayed up there for over an hour and used up two rolls of film.

By the time we came back down into the square we were rather disappointed to find that nearly all the water had drained away and that St Mark's was gradually returning to normal. People were no longer walking in single file on the duckboards but were criss-crossing the square in all directions. Large groups of tourists were being herded along by impatient guides and the professional photographers were eagerly taking pictures of children who were feeding the unbelievably tame pigeons. Aroung the edge of the square shopkeepers and waiters were mopping out the water-logged boutiques and cafes.

ANALYSIS

Creating the right impression

Last year we had a very nice holiday in Ibiza.
Last year we had a lovely holiday in Ibiza.

Which of the sentences above do you prefer? Why?

You can give the reader a stronger, more vivid impression of your personal experiences by using more powerful adjectives. For example, **wonderful** creates a stronger impression than **very good; incredible** is more powerful than **rather surprising** and **exhausting** is more vivid than **extremely tiring.**

Avoiding repetition

It is also important to use a variety of adjectives in your writing. For example, **superb**, **fantastic**, **excellent**, **tremendous** and **wonderful** all have more or less the same meaning. 'Variety is the spice of life' also applies to your writing.

Complete the following with adjectives from both parts of Composition 1.

1 .... and .... both mean **very nice.**

2 .... and .... both mean **very cold.**

3 .... , ... , ... ,
.... and .... all mean **very attractive.**

4 .... means **very bright.**

Simultaneous actions

In the second paragraph of the second part of Composition 1 Michael describes the scene in St Mark's Square when they come out of the basilica.

Notice the repeated use of the past continuous tense (**were criss-crossing**, **were being herded**, **were** eagerly **taking**, **were feeding** and **were mopping out**).

Why do you think these verbs are all in the past continuous tense?

PRACTICE

Exercise 3

Using your imagination, complete the following description of a scene in a French fishing village.

COMPOSITION 2

We decided to stop for lunch at a small port called Le Tréport. We parked the car on the seafront opposite a row of busy-looking restaurants. However, we were all feeling extremely stiff after four hours of non-stop driving so we decided to take a walk along the seafront to the harbour first. How lovely it was to breathe in the sea air once again!

At the harbour there was a lot of activity. Three small fishing boats had just come in and the fishermen ....

The owners of the local restaurants had come to meet the boats and ....

....

There were also a few tourists like ourselves who had come over to see what was going on. Some ....

....

while others ....

Above the boats the seagulls ....

Perhaps they ....

Outside the café opposite the boats, a group of old men ....

.... and ....

The café was very quiet as it was lunch-time and the waiter ....

....

From an open window next to the café came the smell of grilled fish. Somebody was obviously ....

....

By now we were beginning to feel rather hungry and made our way back along the seafront towards the restaurants.

GUIDED WRITING

Composition task

Below is an extract from Richard's diary.

Imagine that you are Richard. Using the information in the diary, describe what happened when you went to London for a rock concert. Write between 120 and 180 words.

COMPOSITION 3

1987 SATURDAY 15 AUGUST

Jan & I left Manchester 8.00 a.m.– PLAN: hitch-hike to London for Springsteen concert tickets 3 weeks before – £15 each! – so not enough money left for train fares

bus to M6 motorway – only hitching 2 minutes – lorry stopped – driver going to Spain via London – what luck! 1·30 p.m.– got to London – tube to Tony's flat in Camden Town – late lunch

drove to Wembley – got to stadium LATE, at 8.15 – traffic terrible! tickets said concert at 8.00 – but no music playing so hadn't missed anything – Springsteen late too – lucky for us! eventually found our seats – FANTASTIC view of stage! now 8·30 but STILL no Springsteen – crowd getting impatient, whistling, slow handclapping – man on stage explained reason for delay – technical problems! 8.45 – lights went out – band started playing – cheering – clapping – SPRINGSTEEN ran on – AT LAST!

11·30 – concert ended – 3 encores – Springsteen superb – crowd delighted – Jan said it was best concert ever – we all agreed

9 Directed writing exercises (2)

PRESENTATION

In Section B of Paper 3, Use of English, you will be asked to do a directed writing exercise.
In the following exercises you are asked to make choices based on the available information and to justify them.

First, study the directed writing exercise on the opposite page and then look at the analysis below.

ANALYSIS

Below, in note form, are the most important points which determine what John and Linda will decide to do and the factors which will help them to choose.

NAME(S)		CHOICE
John and Linda		hire a video
PERSONAL DETAILS		ADVERTISEMENT
① very keen on films (and plays) (often went before Tom was born)	→	Video Palace have an enormous selection of films
② Linda does not want to leave Tom with a babysitter yet	→	can watch films in the comfort of your own home
③ can spend £3.00 each (haven't got much money at the moment	→	even most expensive films can be hired for less than £6.00 per day

The following people are considering what to do this Saturday.

Look at the four advertisements on the right. Then, using the information given in the personal details, continue the four paragraphs below, saying what you think they will decide to do. Write about 50 words for each paragraph.

Name	**Age**	**Details**
John Carter Linda Carter	26 24	married with 2-month-old baby boy, Tom; Linda gave up well-paid job when she had Tom; at the moment finding it difficult to live on John's salary; (1) used to go out to cinema and theatre a lot before baby born; (2) Linda thinks it's too soon to leave Tom with babysitter; (3) can only afford to spend £3.00 each
Daniella Cucina	25	single; works as dancer with 'Hot Shoe' modern ballet company; earns a lot of money; loves going out with her friends at weekends to cinema, theatre and pop concerts; has great sense of humour; not very keen on serious films or plays; prefers straightforward light entertainment; would spend up to £10.00
Patrick Green Sheila Green	66 62	married; both retired last year; living on old age pension of £45.00 per week; have some savings for holidays and emergencies; both enjoy all kinds of classical music; have lots of records; rarely go to concerts, opera or ballet – tickets very expensive; can spend £3.50 each
Julian Sutcliffe	18	single; left school two months ago; working as waiter in Kensington Hotel; all meals and accommodation free; plenty of spending money; loves modern music, especially rock; buys two albums a week; can't stand classical music; Saturday is his day off; prepared to spend up to £10.00

1 I think John and Linda will decide to ....

....

....

2 Daniella Cucina will probably ....

....

....

3 The best choice for Patrick and Sheila would be ....

....

....

4 I expect Julian will ....

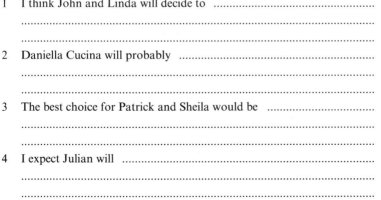

....

....

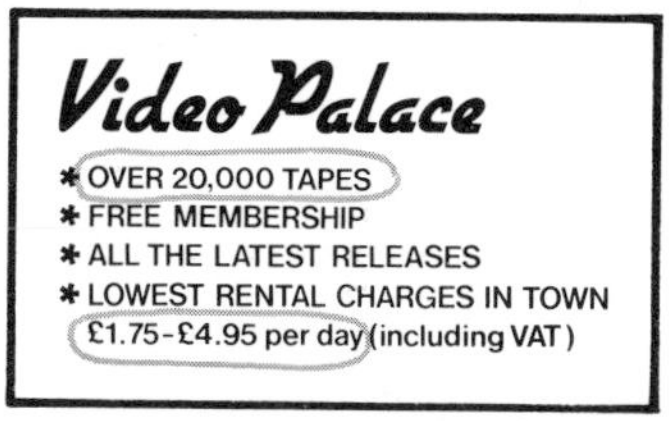

Notice that, where possible, the ideas have been expressed using different words from those underlined in the personal details and ringed in the advertisement.
Your paragraphs should not contain too many direct quotations from the text.

1 *I think John and Linda will decide to ... hire a video for three reasons. (1) The first is that we know that they are very keen on films and that it is possible to hire an enormous selection of films from Video Palace. (2) The second reason is that since Linda does not want to leave Tom with a babysitter it would be better for them to stay at home. (3) Finally, even the most expensive films cost less than £6.00 a day so they would not have to spend more than £3.00 each.*

Linking ideas

Notice the following stylistic features.

1 the use of connectors (**and, since, so**) to link clauses
2 the use of connectors and connecting phrases (**The first is that, The second reason is that, Finally**) to link sentences

(See the lists on page 28 for more examples of connectors and connecting phrases.)

PRACTICE

Exercise 1

1 *With a pencil, underline the most important points in the personal details of Daniella, Patrick and Sheila, and Julian and ring those in each advertisement.*
2 *Write down the person(s) and their choice of entertainment and then underneath write the important points from both the personal details and the advertisement opposite each other, as in the example on page 62. Use your own words where possible.*
3 *Develop your notes so as to complete paragraphs 2, 3 and 4 in about 50 words each.*

Exercise 2

DIRECTED WRITING EXERCISE 2

The following four people have all been asked to attend an interview for the job in the advertisement on the next page.

1 *Read the advertisement and study the information about the four applicants for the job.*

2 *In pairs, discuss each applicant's suitability for the job and make a list of*
   a his/her good points
   b his/her bad points

3 *With a different partner, decide which of the four applicants should be offered the job, giving reasons for your choice.*

4 *When you have finished, compare your choice with those of the other students.*

TOUR GUIDE

reqd. for June, July and August. Based in Edinburgh, s/he will accompany tourists on sightseeing trips around Edinburgh and on tours around the Scottish Highlands. The successful candidate will be outgoing, energetic, unflappable, highly efficient and fluent in at least two of the following:- German, Italian and French – relevant experience preferred but not essential. £150 per week plus free board and lodging. Apply in writing to Mr B Connolly, PO Box 6MP, Edinburgh

APPLICANT 1

Stewart Wells – 20 – 2nd year student at Oxford University – studying German language and literature – bilingual in English and Italian as his mother is from Naples, Italy – comes from Edinburgh – has worked in hotels and restaurants during university holidays

APPLICANT 2

Corinne Hamilton-Jones – 24 – unemployed actress – worked for years for the Scottish Tourist Board in Glasgow after leaving school – spent 9 months in France as an au-pair 2 years ago – is studying Spanish at night school – also speaks some German as her current boyfriend is Austrian

APPLICANT 3

Jamie McDougall – 34 – courier for Rainbow Holidays – presently working in Tunisia where he has to speak mainly French – has also worked for periods of 4–5 months in Greece, Austria, Mexico and France – originally from Aberdeen, Scotland – would like to find a permanent job in the travel industry in Scotland

APPLICANT 4

Heidi Muller – 27 – German teacher at Goethe Institute in London – comes from Berne, Switzerland – has been living in the UK for 6 years – is married to an American businessman – bilingual in German and French – her husband has been offered a job working in the oil industry in Aberdeen so they are moving to Scotland

9

ANALYSIS

Text organisation

The sentences below have been taken from **two** separate paragraphs and placed in the wrong order. The two paragraphs are part of the answer to a directed writing exercise which consists of choosing the best ways of travelling from London to Liverpool for four different people.

In pairs, put the sentences in the correct order and then write out the two separate paragraphs.

a Finally, it would probably be useful to have the car in Liverpool as they may wish to go out in it somewhere and they would not all fit into David's parents' car.
b Therefore, he would not have to leave London until eight o'clock.
c Consequently, he would need to leave very early in the morning and would probably be rather tired when he arrived.
d I think John Davis will go by British Rail because he needs to be in Liverpool at eleven o'clock for his interview and the train only takes two and a half hours.
e Secondly, David and his family are going to Liverpool for several days so they will probably not mind having a four-hour car journey.
f It would be best for David to travel by car because, in the first place, it would only cost £18.00 for the whole family to travel there and back.
g Lastly, the train is not as cheap as the coach but he need not worry about the cost as the company will pay his expenses.
h If, on the other hand, he went by coach or by car it would take four or five hours to get there.
i This would work out at £4.50 per person, which would be far cheaper than either the coach or the train.

PRACTICE

Exercise 3

Using the connector in brackets, re-write each of the following sentences so that its meaning remains the same.

In some cases you will need to change the order of the words. In other cases it will be necessary to make two sentences where previously there was one, or to join two sentences together.

e.g. ... **since** Linda does not want to leave Tom with a babysitter it would be better for them to stay at home. (so)
Linda does not want to leave Tom with a babysitter **so** it would be better for them to stay at home.

1 ... even the most expensive films cost less than £6.00 a day **so** they would not have to spend more than £3.00 each. (because)
2 I think John Davis will go by British Rail **because** he needs to be in Liverpool at eleven o'clock for his interview ... (as)
3 ... the train only takes two and a half hours. **Therefore**, he would not have to leave London until eight o'clock. (since)
4 ... it would take four or five hours to get there. **Consequently**, he would need to leave very early in the morning. (because)
5 ... he need not worry about the cost **as** the company will pay his expenses. (so)
6 It would be best for David to travel by car **because** it would only cost £18.00 for the whole family to travel there and back. (therefore)
7 ... David and his family are going to Liverpool for several days **so** they will probably not mind having a four-hour car journey. (consequently)
8 ... it would probably be useful to have the car in Liverpool **as** they may wish to go out in it somewhere. (so)

Exercise 4

First read the two paragraphs below, which give reasons to support the writer's choice of restaurants, and then fill in the gaps, using a variety of connectors and connecting phrases. (See the lists on page 28.)

1 In my opinion John and Pat should go to La Dolce Vita restaurant .... they have been there before .... they know the food is always of a high standard. .... , they spent their honeymoon in Rome .... it would be romantic to celebrate their wedding anniversary in an Italian restaurant. Another .... they ought to go to La Dolce Vita is that .... it is only five minutes' walk from their flat they would not need to take their car. .... , both of them could drink without having to worry about driving home. .... , the restaurant now has a few tables in its garden .... they would be able to eat in the open air if it was a nice evening.

2 I think that Nigel should take Samantha to Le Petit Prince restaurant for a number of reasons. .... , a friend of his told him that Samantha liked French food .... she rarely eats out in restaurants .... nurses' salaries are so low. .... , the restaurant is recommended in the *1987 Good Food Guide* .... the food ought to be very good. .... , customers are allowed to bring their own wine .... Nigel would be able to take the bottle of champagne that he has bought to celebrate Samantha's birthday.

GUIDED WRITING

Composition task

Read the following passages about the discovery of some drugs at a youth centre in Arlington and look at the instructions on page 69.

Use the following technique to help you.

1 Read the newspaper cutting, the two letters and the press release and then decide whether you agree most with Reginald or with Dennis.
2 Read through the passages again, underlining any points which support the point of view you have chosen to represent.
3 Using your own words where possible, make notes summarising the main points of your argument.
4 Develop your notes so as to complete the paragraph.

DIRECTED WRITING EXERCISE 3

HEROIN SEIZED AT ALEXANDRA YOUTH CENTRE

LAST NIGHT Arlington police discovered nearly ten grammes of heroin when they carried out a search at The Alexandra Youth Centre in Lauradale Road in Upper Arlington.

Acting on a tip-off from an anonymous informer, police raided the centre at half past nine yesterday evening and searched the forty members and three youth leaders present.

Later three youths were taken to Arlington Police Station where they were charged with possession of heroin. The youths were Steven Atkinson of Honeywell Road, Upper Arlington, Simon Thornton of Wharfedale Crescent, Thackley and Rosemary Goodman of Cherry Tree Avenue, Upper Arlington. The youths will appear before Arlington magistrates this afternoon.

Last night's discovery of drugs at The Alexandra will add weight to the arguments of the Lauradale Residents' Association, who have been campaigning for the closure of the centre since its opening in 1982.

Sir

I am writing to express my deep concern about recent developments at The Alexandra Youth Centre.

The Lauradale Residents' Association were against the idea of building a youth centre in Lauradale Road when the proposal was first put forward in 1980. Our main objection was that the centre would dramatically change the character of this respectable neighbourhood. Unfortunately, the shocking events of the last few days have proved that we were right.

However, even before last week's drug scandal, which revealed that the Alexandra was the centre of a massive drugs ring, local residents have had many reasons to complain about this youth centre. First, there is the constant noise, not only from the ear-splitting discos and concerts, which keep our children awake at night, but also from the endless procession of motorbikes up and down our (previously quiet) roads until long after midnight. Second, the groups of shouting, swearing and aggressive teenagers who hang around on our street corners at all hours have made the area a much less pleasant place in which to live. Local children have been terrorised, walls have been covered in obscene graffiti, residents' cars have been scratched and the phone box has been continually vandalised. And now, to make matters even worse, we learn that The Alexandra has become a haven for drug pushers and heroin addicts!

Consequently, I feel most strongly, and I know that the vast majority of local residents agree with me, that The Alexandra Youth Centre should be closed down immediately.

Reginald Remington, Chairman,
Lauradale Residents' Association

Sir

I am writing to reply to Reginald Remington's letter, which you published on July 18th.

First and foremost, I would like to point out that this is the first time in the five years since it opened that The Alexandra has ever been connected in any way with drugs. What is more, to call the discovery of a few grammes of heroin a 'drugs scandal' and to claim that The Alexandra is 'the centre of a massive drugs ring' is typical of the kind of hysterical reaction that we have come to expect from Reginald Remington and his supporters. In a club with over 200 members, 90% of whom are unemployed, it is hardly surprising that one or two individuals should sometimes get themselves into trouble with the law. However, I feel that it would be quite wrong to close The Alexandra because of the foolish behaviour of three people.

Furthermore, the centre serves an extremely important role in the local community by providing important cultural and leisure facilities for Arlington's largely unemployed school-leavers. We have also encouraged many of our members to take part in valuable community projects such as building children's adventure playgrounds, visiting old people and accompanying handicapped children on day visits to the seaside.

Therefore, The Alexandra must remain open, despite the unfortunate events of the past week. The whole of Arlington needs its youth centre, perhaps more than it realises.

Dennis Mitchell, Leader,
The Alexandra Youth Centre

ALEXANDRA YOUTH CENTRE

PRESS RELEASE

On Saturday, 25th July 1987, over 200 local people demonstrated their support for The Alexandra Youth Centre by signing a petition which was presented yesterday to the leader of Arlington Council, Tony Braithwaite. The petition urged the council to do everything within its power to ensure that the centre remains open.

Yesterday Dennis Mitchell, Leader of The Alexandra Youth Centre said, 'We completely deny the claims that have been made in the local press over the past week that the centre has been used as an outlet for the distribution of drugs.'

Mr Mitchell also pointed out the The Alexandra had always enjoyed a good relationship with the local police force as well as with the community as a whole.

ENDS

For further information contact:

Dennis Mitchell
The Alexandra Youth Centre
Lauradale Road
Arlington AG2 6BC
Tel: 0721 - 806624

NOTES FOR EDITORS

1 The Alexandra was opened by HRH Princess Diana in June 1982.
2 Leisure facilities provided by the centre include library, snack bar, table-tennis tables, snooker tables, television room, drama workshop, film projection room, photographic darkroom, pottery workshop and music room.
3 The petition was signed by 204 local residents in Wood Lane, Cherry Tree Avenue and Lauradale Road.

Reginald Remington and Dennis Mitchell have very different opinions about what should happen to The Alexandra Youth Centre.

Who do you agree with most?

Complete the following paragraph in about 100 words, giving your reasons for supporting either Reginald or Dennis's point of view.

I agree most with ....
because ....
....

10 Informal letters (2)

PRESENTATION

Read the following letter, in which Graham invites Simon to go on holiday with him.

LETTER 1

41 Addison Road
Bradford
BD10 8QS
3rd March 1987

Dear Simon,

Thanks for the birthday card and accompanying letter. It was so nice to hear all your news. I've been meaning to write to you for ages but somehow just haven't been able to find the time.

Anyway, I had a lovely birthday. Paula, Mark, Brian, Sally, Keith and I had an enormous meal at a new Italian restaurant which has just opened in town, Viareggio I think it's called, and after that we went on to a disco in Leeds. What a shame you couldn't come back to Bradford for that weekend!

You know in your letter you were wondering if I had made any holiday plans for the summer. Well, Paula's uncle and aunt in Cornwall have just asked her if she'd like to go and stay down there for two weeks so that she can look after their cottage for them while they're away on holiday in the States. They've said that she could bring three or four friends too, since it's quite big and there are four bedrooms.

Apparently, the cottage is out in the country so we'd be able to go on lots of long walks. What's more, it's only about fifteen minutes by car to the coast, so it'd be handy for the beach too, weather permitting. Sounds to me like a really good idea for a holiday, especially as the accommodation wouldn't cost us a penny!

Anyway, think about it and let me know whether you're interested in coming along. Paula's relatives are planning to go on holiday to the States at the beginning of August, so you've got plenty of time to consider it.

Well, I'd better finish off now because I'm playing squash with Brian in half an hour. I still haven't managed to beat him, you know!

Hope to see you soon,
All the best,
Graham

ANALYSIS

Linking ideas

Using the underlined words to help you, complete the following sentences about the letter opposite.

1 Graham hasn't written to Simon recently because ....

2 Viareggio is ....

3 Paula's uncle and aunt have invited her to Cornwall for two weeks to ....
....

4 During those two weeks they will be ....

5 The cottage is quite big so Paula ....

6 It's right out in the country and it's ....

7 Graham's playing squash in half an hour so ....

PRACTICE

Exercise 1

Link each of the following pairs or groups of sentences together using one of the connectors underlined in Letter 1.
In some cases you will need to omit certain words or change the word order.

e.g. It was so nice to see you last weekend. It was lovely to see the children, too.
It was so nice to see you **and** the children last weekend.

1 It's ages since I've written to you. I just thought I'd drop you a line to let you know how I am getting on.
2 I've agreed to babysit for my sister on the Saturday evening. She'll be able to go out and celebrate her wedding anniversary.
3 Right, I'd better stop now. I have to go and pick up the children from school.
4 I don't think you've been to Edinburgh before. I've drawn you a map showing you how to get to our house from the end of the motorway.
5 I was in Spain last summer. I learned a great deal of Spanish. I learned a few words of Catalan, too.
6 I think I'll probably come over in the car. Then I won't have to catch the last train home.
7 I'd love to be able to put you up when you come down to Oxford. Unfortunately, I've already arranged for my brother to stay with us for those two days.
8 We thought it would be nice to throw a surprise party for Grandma. It's her eightieth birthday on Sunday. We've invited all the immediate family over.

10

ANALYSIS

Text organisation

The sentences in the letter below are in the wrong order.

1 *In pairs, put them in the correct order (1–13) and decide where the letter should be divided into paragraphs.*

LETTER 2

17a Lyndhurst Terrace
London NW3 6BU

12th October 1987

Dear Paul

a Now, as for the flat itself, I've made up the bed for you in the spare room so you won't need to bring a sleeping-bag. ☐

b She'll be working nights at the hospital next week so you'll have to pick them up by seven at the latest, which is when she sets off for work. ☐

c This is just a short note to let you know what arrangements I've made for you to stay in the flat next week. ☐

d The first is to water all the plants at least once while you're there, preferably towards the end of the week. ☐

e Incidentally, you'll find the central heating controls in the same cupboard, on the right-hand wall next to the hot water tank. ☐

f By the way, I wonder if you could remember to do a couple of things for me during your stay? ☐

g You can't miss it. It's the enormous building on your right as you walk up the hill from the tube station. ☐

h Well, I think that's about everything. ☐

i If you find you're not warm enough at night, there are some extra blankets in the airing cupboard in the bathroom. ☐

j If, for any reason, you get there after that time, she'll leave them with the receptionist at the hospital. ☐

k Have a good week in London and thanks again for 'flatsitting'! ☐

l And the other is to make sure that you close all the windows and double-lock the door when you go out. ☐

m I've arranged to leave the keys with the girl in the flat upstairs, Diane, who works at the Royal Free Hospital. ☐

With love from

Jane

2 *When you have finished, look at each sentence again and indicate which words link it to the preceding sentence(s) and which words link it to the following sentence(s).*

e.g. By the way, I wonder if you could remember to do (a couple of things) for me during your stay? (The first) is to water all the plants at least once while you're there … And (the other) is to …

PRACTICE

Exercise 2

In pairs, re-write the letter below, using the words in brackets to help you.

Pay special attention to the following:

LAYOUT Are the address, date and salutation correct and in the right position?
STRUCTURE Is it divided into paragraphs in the appropriate places?
STYLE Are the ideas linked together by suitable connectors?
Has the unnecessary repetition of nouns been avoided by the use of pronouns? (See page 34.)

LETTER 3

Rose Cottage, Long Melford, Suffolk

10th July 1987

Dear Rachel,

1 Just thought I'd write you a few lines. I'd like to say how much I enjoyed staying with you in London last weekend. (to) **2** It was great to go to so many interesting places. It was great to do so many different things, too. (and) **3** I'd love to come and stay with you in London again some time. Is that all right with you? (if) **4** Chris got a bit of a shock. I told Chris that I'd spent over £150 in two days. I shouldn't think Chris will want me to come and stay with you in London too often! (when, so) **5** Chris said he liked the yellow dress. You persuaded me to buy the yellow dress in that beautiful little shop in Covent Garden. Chris said that he didn't understand why I wanted another dress! (which, but) There's such a lovely, relaxing atmosphere in Covent Garden, isn't there? **6** I especially enjoyed sitting outside that café. We had those enormous cream cakes. We also listened to that man playing the saxophone. (where, and) **7** That man reminded me of Robert De Niro in *New York, New York.* We saw *New York, New York* together. We were at university. (which, when) **8** I'll have to come up to London again soon. We can go and see another play together at the theatre. (so) **9** *The Gambler* was the first play I've been to for over five years. That's a long time, isn't it? (which) **10** I thought *The Gambler* was extremely funny. I also thought the four actors in *The Gambler* were all superb. (and that) Anyway, thanks again for a marvellous weekend. **11** Let's try and write to each other more often from now on. Then we won't lose touch again. (so) All my love.

Sarah

Exercise 3

Below is the letter that Paul wrote to Jane to thank her for letting him stay in her flat in London while she was away on holiday.

First read Paul's letter and then fill in the gaps and write a suitable last paragraph. Use Letter 1 and Letter 2 to help you.

LETTER 4

Dear Jane,

.... your flat while you were away on holiday. I expect you're looking disgustingly tanned and healthy after a week in the sun. It's all right for some, isn't it?

.... , the reason I'm writing, as I'm sure you've guessed, is to .... breaking the antique Chinese vase .... was on the chest of drawers by the window in my bedroom.

This is how it happened: .... I got back to the flat on the Monday evening I realised that I didn't have the door keys on me. You see, I'd left the flat in rather a hurry that morning .... I didn't want to be late for my first appointment. So in my hurry to leave I must have forgotten to put .... in my pocket. At first I thought the nurse upstairs might have a spare key, ... , unfortunately, it was half past seven .... she had already left for work.

In the end I thought the best thing to do would be to try and get into the flat through a window. Luckily, I'd forgotten to close the one in my bedroom that morning .... I was able to get in without having to break any of the window panes. However, it was .... dark on that side of the building that I couldn't see anything in the bedroom at all. Unfortunately, ... I was climbing through the window I knocked the vase with my foot and .... fell onto the floor .... smashed into pieces. For a moment I was afraid that one of the neighbours might think there was a burglar in your flat .... , luckily for me, nobody seemed to hear it.

....
....
....

.... Paul

GUIDED WRITING

Composition task

Below is a wedding invitation addressed to Barry, a friend of the bride and groom, and a map which shows the location of the church and the restaurant.

Imagine that you are either Jennifer or Adam and write a letter to accompany the official invitation, using the structure suggested below.

LETTER 5

Paragraph 1	Invite Barry to your wedding.
Paragraph 2	Explain how to get to the church and the restaurant.
Paragraph 3	Give more details about the reception.
Paragraph 4	Recommend a hotel for him to stay at.
Paragraph 5	Express your hope that he will be able to come.

Date the letter 25th May 1987 and write between 120 and 180 words.

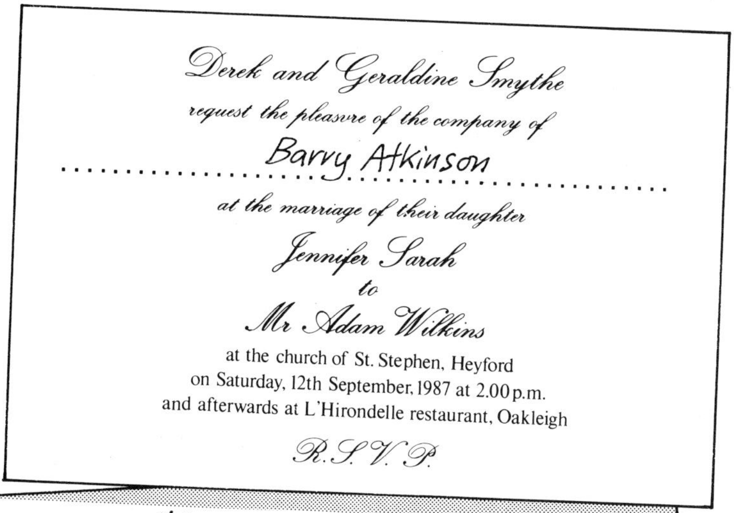

Derek and Geraldine Smythe
request the pleasure of the company of
Barry Atkinson
at the marriage of their daughter
Jennifer Sarah
to
Mr Adam Wilkins
at the church of St. Stephen, Heyford
on Saturday, 12th September, 1987 at 2.00 p.m.
and afterwards at L'Hirondelle restaurant, Oakleigh
R.S.V.P.

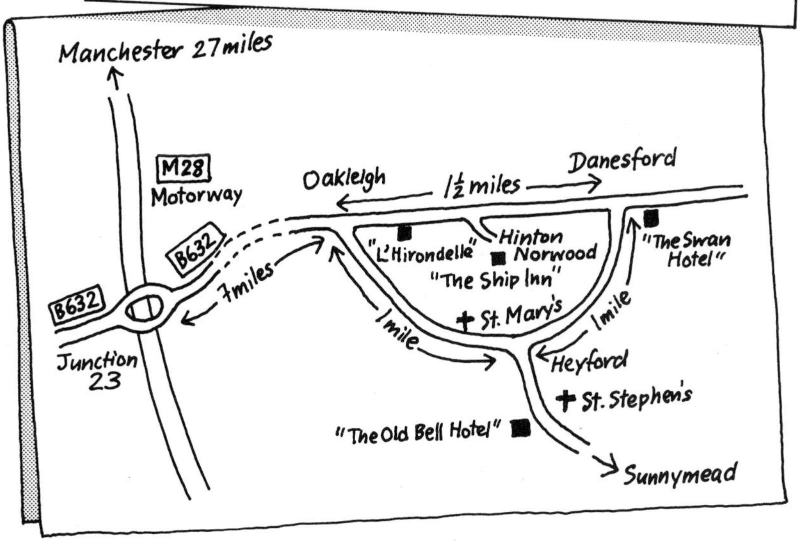

11 Discursive essays (3)

PRESENTATION

Read the following essay about why so many young people are taking drugs these days and what can be done about this problem.

ESSAY 1

> The number of young people taking hard drugs such as heroin and cocaine has increased enormously in recent years.
> Why do you think more and more young people are turning to drugs these days? What do you think can be done about this problem?

In my view a lot more young people take drugs these days because they are unemployed and so they feel bored and depressed. Many young people without work do not know what to do with all their free time and often feel very pessimistic about the chances of finding a job in the future. Therefore, some of them turn to drugs to relieve the boredom and depression of their lives.

It seems to me that there are several ways of dealing with this problem. In the first place, I feel that the government ought to make sure that all young people out of work have some kind of full-time occupation. For example, they could attend training centres to learn a profession or take part in community work such as looking after old people. If these young people were fully occupied, they would not get so bored or depressed and would not need to take drugs.

Secondly, I think that there should be more customs officers at airports and ports. This would stop people from bringing drugs into the country.

In addition, it would be a good idea to create more drug squads in the police force. If these squads were able to catch more drug traffickers, they could reduce the quantity of drugs on the market.

Another solution would be to give more severe punishments to people convicted of drug trafficking. This would probably deter many people from smuggling or selling drugs.

Finally, I feel that the government should warn people about the dangers of taking drugs. If young people realised how seriously drugs can damage their health, fewer people would want to take them.

ANALYSIS

Text organisation

Notice that there is neither an introductory nor a concluding paragraph in the essay above. This is because the subject of the essay is introduced in the question itself and because it is unnecessary to repeat all of the writer's suggestions at the end.

There are six paragraphs in the essay.

1 *Complete the following summary of the first paragraph.*

Paragraph 1 The writer answers the first part of the question.

He/she thinks that the increase in drug taking has happened because ....

....

2 *Complete the table below, which shows the organisation of ideas in paragraphs 2 to 6.*

The writer's solutions to the drug problem		
Paragraph	Word or phrase which introduces each suggestion	Suggestions
2	....	all young people should be fully occupied
3	Secondly	....
4	....	....
5	....	more severe penalities for drug traffickers
6	Finally	....

Useful language

OPINIONS

Find four phrases in Essay 1 which have the same meaning as ***in my opinion****.*

1 ....

2 ....

3 ....

4 ....

SUGGESTIONS

In my opinion the government **should** spend more money on education.

The writer of Essay 1 has made suggestions like the one above using two other constructions.

Find these two constructions in the essay and re-write the sentence above using each construction once.

1 ....

2 ....

Linking ideas

Using the underlined words to help you, complete the following sentences about Essay 1.

1 The writer feels that young unemployed people who had a full-time occupation would not take drugs because ....

2 If there were more customs officials at airports and ports, people ....

3 The writer suggests creating more drug squads to catch drug traffickers. This would ....

4 People would be deterred from trafficking if ....

5 The writer thinks that it would be a good idea for the government to tell the public more about the dangers of drug abuse. This would ....

PRACTICE

Exercise 1

1 *In pairs, discuss what you think could be done about each of the problems below and note down some possible solutions to each one.*

a Unemployment is a serious problem in most European countries these days.
b Millions of people in developing countries do not have enough to eat.
c The Earth's oil supplies will have run out by the middle of the twenty-first century.
d Our rivers and seas are becoming more and more polluted.
e The majority of traffic accidents are caused by drivers who have been drinking alcohol.

2 *For each problem choose two of your solutions and write a paragraph about each solution, explaining why it would be a good idea. Use phrases and constructions like those* ***highlighted*** *in the following example.*

e.g. PROBLEM
Every year thousands of cyclists are involved in road accidents.
POSSIBLE SOLUTIONS
cycle lanes, riding tests for cyclists, advertising campaign to make drivers more aware of cyclists, compulsory helmets for cyclists

Paragraph 1 **I think that** the government **should** create more cycle lanes in our cities. **If** there **were** more cycle lanes, it **would reduce** the number of accidents involving cyclists.

Paragraph 2 **In my opinion** the government **ought to** make cyclists take riding tests. **This would improve** the standard of cycling and help to keep the number of cycling accidents down.

ANALYSIS

Text organisation

The sentences in the essay below are in the wrong order.

In pairs, put them in the correct order (1–9) and decide where the essay should be divided into paragraphs.

ESSAY 2

During the 1980s there has been a dramatic increase in the number of airliners which have been hijacked by fanatical terrorist groups.
What measures could the authorities take to prevent future hijacks?

a These would be armed airline security guards who would travel on planes disguised as ordinary passengers. ☐

b This may result in some casualties among the passengers and cabin crew but it might eventually stop terrorists from thinking that they can achieve their aims by hijacking airliners. ☐

c Also, it would be a good thing to increase security all around the outside of airports so that terrorists could not get into airports by climbing over perimeter fences or by pretending to be airport staff. ☐

d Lastly, I believe that governments should refuse to give in to the demands of terrorists and should be prepared to use force to defeat the hijackers and to free their hostages. ☐

e Besides these measures to improve security at airports, I would also be in favour of the idea of having 'sky marshalls' on board all airliners. ☐

f Then, if any of the passengers tried to take control of the airliner during the flight, the 'sky marshalls' would probably be able to stop the hijack attempt. ☐

g To begin with, I think that there ought to be more security staff and better detection equipment inside airports to search passengers and their luggage. ☐

h In my opinion, there are several things the authorities could do in order to prevent terrorists from hijacking airliners. ☐

i This would make it much more difficult for hijackers to smuggle weapons and explosives onto airliners. ☐

11

GUIDED WRITING

Essay planning

In pairs, first consider the following essay questions and then note down four possible solutions and their consequences.

1 During the last ten years there has been a large increase in the number of burglaries in our cities.
What do you think could be done to reduce the number of burglaries?

	SOLUTIONS	CONSEQUENCES
1	improve locks on doors and windows	make it more difficult for burglars to get in
2	....	....
3	....	....
4	....	....

2 Most doctors believe that smoking is directly responsible for serious, often fatal diseases such as lung cancer and heart disease.
What steps could be taken to discourage people from smoking?

	SOLUTIONS	CONSEQUENCES
1	....	....
2	....	....
3	....	....
4	....	....

3 There are now enough nuclear weapons in the world to destroy our planet many times over. How do you think the number of nuclear weapons could be reduced?

SOLUTIONS	CONSEQUENCES
1	....
....	....
2	....
....	....
3	....
....	....
4	....
....	....

4 Disabled people often feel as if they are separated from the community in which they live. What could be done to integrate the disabled more into our communities?

SOLUTIONS	CONSEQUENCES
1	....
....	....
2	....
....	....
3	....
....	....
4	....
....	....

Composition task

Choose one of the essay topics above and write an essay of between 120 and 180 words, using the structure suggested below.

ESSAY 3

Paragraph 1 State that in your opinion there are several solutions to the problem. Give your first suggestion and explain why it would be a good idea.
Paragraph 2 Give your second suggestion and explain why it would be a good idea.
Paragraph 3 Give your third suggestion and explain why it would be a good idea.
Paragraph 4 Give your final suggestion and explain why it would be a good idea.

12 Biographical essays

PRESENTATION

Read the following description of the life of George Orwell, one of the best British writers of the twentieth century.

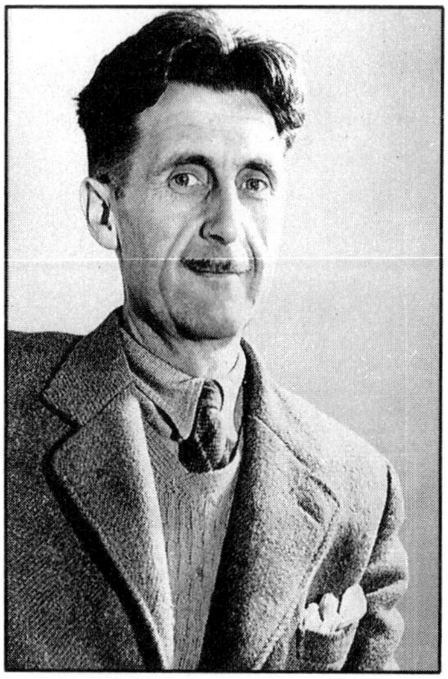

COMPOSITION 1

George Orwell, **whose** real name was Eric Blair, was born **in 1903** in Bengal, India, **where** his father was working for the British Civil Service.

In 1907 the family returned to England and **when he was fourteen** Orwell won a scholarship to Eton College, one of the most famous public schools in the country. It was **here** that he began his career as a writer by contributing to college magazines.

When Orwell left Eton **in 1921** he decided not to go to university. Instead he went to India **the following year** and joined the Indian Imperial Police in Burma, **where** he remained **until 1928.**

After returning to England he decided that he wanted to find out for himself what it was like to be really poor. So **for the next two years** he deliberately lived in extreme poverty in Paris, **where** he worked as a dish-washer, and in England, **where** for a while he lived as a tramp.

In the early 1930s he worked **first** as a teacher and **later** as a part-time assistant in a London bookshop. **It was during this period** that he started writing. *Down and Out in Paris and London,* **which** was an account of his experiences of living in poverty, was published **in 1933.**

At the end of 1936 Orwell went to Spain, **where** he was wounded **while fighting** for the Republicans in the Spanish Civil War. As a result of his experiences in Spain as a socialist militiaman, **which** are described in *Homage to Catalonia* (1938), he became extremely critical of Communism.

During the Second World War Orwell worked for the BBC Indian Service and **later** became the Literary Editor of *Tribune* and war correspondent for the *Observer.*

Although he had been regarded as one of our leading authors **since 1938**, Orwell remained poor **until his death** in 1950 **at the age of forty-six**. He had been suffering from tuberculosis **for many years**.

His best-known novels are *Animal Farm* (1945) and *Nineteen Eighty-Four* (1949). **The former** is a savage attack on Stalinism, in the form of a political fable, while **the latter** is a terrifying vision of a world in the future, **in which** England is under the control of an all-powerful, totalitarian régime.

ANALYSIS

Ordering events

There are nine paragraphs in the composition opposite and each one corresponds to an event or period in Orwell's life.

Put the following sentences, which summarise the nine paragraphs, in the correct order (1–9).

- **a** He fought in the Spanish Civil War. ☐
- **b** He joined the Indian Imperial Police in Burma. ☐
- **c** He started writing. ☐
- **d** He was born in Bengal, India. ☐
- **e** He died in 1950. ☐
- **f** He worked as a journalist. ☐
- **g** He lived in poverty in Paris and England. ☐
- **h** He was educated at Eton. ☐
- **i** He wrote *Animal Farm* and *Nineteen Eighty-Four*. ☐

Linking ideas

*Using the **highlighted** words to help you, complete the following sentences about Composition 1.*

1 Orwell's father was working for the Civil Service in ....

2 When he was .... his family came back to England.

3 In .... Orwell went to Eton.

4 While he was .... he wrote for the college magazines.

5 Orwell left school when he was ....

6 In .... he joined the Indian Imperial Police.

7 In 1928 Orwell ....

8 From 1928 .... he chose to live in extreme poverty in Paris and in London.

9 Before working as a bookshop assistant he ....

10 Orwell wrote about his experiences as a dish-washer and as a tramp in ....
.... (1933).

11 He was wounded during ....

12 *Homage to Catalonia* is about ....

13 After the Second World War he was ....

14 Orwell was only .... when he died in 1950.

15 '..' is a political fable attacking Stalinism.

16 '..' is a frightening vision of life in the future.

12

Useful language

Billie, **who** had been an addict for many years, finally died from drug abuse in 1959, at the age of forty-four.

Billie Holiday, **whose** real name was Eleanor Gough McKay, was born in Baltimore on April 7th, 1915.

Later Billie and her mother moved to New York, **where** she began her career as a singer in the jazz clubs of Harlem.

The Hollywood film *Lady Sings the Blues*, **which** tells the story of her life, has made Billie Holiday's music extremely popular once again.

PRACTICE

Exercise 1

Link each of the following pairs of sentences together using **who, whose, where** *or* **which.** *In some cases you will need to omit certain words and/or change the order of the information.*

e.g. Diego Maradona was in superb form in 1986 in Mexico. He helped Argentina to win the World Cup for the second time in eight years.

Diego Maradona was in superb form in 1986 in Mexico, **where** he helped Argentina to win the World Cup for the second time in eight years.

1 Che Guevara has been a very close companion of Fidel Castro during the Cuban Revolution. He left Cuba in 1965 to lead a revolutionary guerrilla army in Bolivia.

2 *Guernica* (1937) shows the horrors of the German bombing of a small Basque town during the Spanish Civil War. It is probably Picasso's most famous painting.

3 In November 1963 John F Kennedy was assassinated in Dallas. He had gone to Dallas as part of a pre-election tour around Texas.

4 Orson Welles' best-known films include *The Third Man* and *Citizen Kane.* He died in 1985 at the age of seventy.

5 Luciano Pavarotti had acquired the nickname 'Passion Flower' owing to his passion for women. He married Adua Veroni in 1961.

6 Nelson Mandela's father had fought for the South African Army in the First World War. Mandela was shocked when he found that his school history books always described blacks as either savages or cattle thieves.

7 As soon as the war was over France held presidential elections. These were easily won by General De Gaulle.

8 William Shakespeare was born and brought up in Stratford-Upon-Avon. His father was the mayor of Stratford-Upon-Avon.

ANALYSIS

Useful language

ORDERING EVENTS 1)——— 2)——— 3)———

First he ...
Then he ...
Later he ...
Finally/Eventually he ...

CONNECTING EVENTS —X———|———X—
(before) (event) (after)

Before/After Orwell returned to England he ...
Before/After returning to England he ...
Before/After the Second World War he ...
Two years before/later he ...
The previous/following year he ...

PERIOD (IN TIME) (1922) → (1928)	POINT (IN TIME) × (1921)
Between 1922 and 1928 he ...	In 1921 he ...
From 1922 to/until 1928 he ...	When he was eighteen he ...
In the early 1930s ...	At the age of eighteen he ...
For the next six years he ...	When he left Eton he ...
During the Second World War he ...	
It was during this period/time that he ...	
While (he was) fighting in Spain he ...	

PRACTICE

Exercise 2

*First read the following description of the life of Martin Luther King and then fill in the gaps with either a suitable relative pronoun (**who, whose, where, which**) or one of the time connectors or connecting phrases below.*

during his final year   eventually   in the following year   on 4 April 1968
between 1951 and 1955   in the early 1960s   after graduating
from 1965 until   while he was studying   at the age of fifteen

COMPOSITION 2

Martin Luther King, ... led the first mass civil rights movement in the USA, was born in 1929 in Atlanta, Georgia, ... his father was a Baptist minister.

.... he entered Morehouse College, Atlanta, ... he studied Medicine and Law. However, ... at the college he decided to enter the ministry, like his father.

.... with a BA in 1948 he studied at the Crozer Theological Seminary in Pennsylvania, ... he became a Bachelor of Divinity in 1951.

.... he attended Boston University. .... there he met Coretta Scott, ... he married in 1953.

In 1955 King became a pastor in Montgomery, Alabama, ... he organised a boycott of the bus company in protest at the racial segregation on the town's buses. .... , after a year-long boycott, the US Supreme Court abolished segregated seating on Montgomery's buses.

In 1957 King helped to found the Southern Christian Leadership Conference, ... organised a series of peaceful protests against racial inequality and segregation all over the South.

.... King became the most influential black civil rights leader in the USA. On 28 August 1963 he led an enormous march to Washington DC, ... was attended by 250,000 people. It was here that he made his famous 'I have a dream' speech.

.... the US Congress passed the 1964 Civil Rights Act, ... abolished segregation in all public places and made racial segregation illegal in all areas of American society. In the same year he received the Nobel Peace Prize for his leadership of the non-violent struggle for racial equality in the USA.

.... his death in 1968 he turned his attentions to the problems facing negroes in the North, ... they lived in the socially deprived ghettos of the large towns.

.... he was assassinated by a sniper in Memphis, Tennessee, ... he had gone to help during a strike of the city's refuse collectors, ... were mostly black.

GUIDED WRITING

Composition task

COMPOSITION 3

Using the information below, write a description of the life of Eva Perón. You need not include all of the information but should make sure that your description contains the most important facts. Write between 120 and 180 words.

Eva Perón

1919 born – Los Toldos – small pampas village in province of Buenos Aires – illegitimate child of Juana Ilbarguren – very poor

1934 went to Buenos Aires – hoped to become a great actress

1935–40 played minor parts in Buenos Aires theatres – acted in inferior films

1942 starred in series of radio soap operas about famous women in history – Queen Elizabeth I, Empress Josephine etc.

1944 became lover of Colonel Imbert, Minister of Communications – persuaded him to organise all-star variety performance – raise money for victims of San Juan earthquake – there met Juan Perón, 48, one of colonels in military government – he soon became vice-president

1945 coup – government overthrown, Perón imprisoned – Eva organised massive demonstration – forced coup leaders to release Perón – reinstated as head of government – Dec 9: Eva married Juan Perón

1946 democratic elections – Perón elected president

1946–50 Eva extremely influential in government – no official position but within 2 years she was practically running Argentina – controlled radio, press and CGT, largest trade union – loved the poor, hated the rich – gave massive pay rises to workers – created Social Aid Foundation (1949) – enormous charity – funded by unions and big business etc. – spent millions on social services (hospitals, schools etc.) – won the hearts of ordinary Argentinians – called her "The Lady of Hope" – but disliked by many rich

1952 July 26 – died of cancer – aged 32 – 2 million people queued to pay last respects to their beloved "Evita"

13 Speeches and talks

PRESENTATION

Read the following speech, which Ian made at his best friend Martin's wedding.

SPEECH 1

"Now, could I have your attention for a few minutes, please? Thank you. Right, first of all, I'd like to thank you all for coming here today to celebrate this wonderful occasion with us. As you know, several people here have had to travel a long way to be with us, particularly Andrew and Denise, who arrived this morning from Switzerland, and I'd like to say a special 'Thank you' to them.

Well, I must admit that I wasn't sure whether Martin would be well enough to come to his wedding when I saw him at ten o'clock this morning. You can't imagine how dreadful he looked! His eyes were red, his face was grey and his tongue was green. At first, I thought that perhaps he was just suffering from last minute nerves, but then I remembered how we had celebrated Martin's last night of freedom together. Fortunately, he felt much better after I helped him take a cold shower and made him drink six cups of strong black coffee! By the way, I hope none of you will tell Carol about Martin's scandalous behaviour at the disco last night. She might not see the funny side of it!

Well, I don't mind telling you that it came as a complete surprise to me when Martin told me that he and Carol were getting married. I mean, they'd only been going out together for eight years, which isn't really long enough to get to know somebody, is it? So, naturally, I told him that he was taking a big risk by marrying somebody he hardly knew and that perhaps they ought to wait a bit longer before finally making up their minds but, as usual, he wouldn't listen to me.

No, seriously, I'm really very glad that Martin didn't pay any attention to me and that he and Carol have finally 'tied the knot' after all this time. I'm quite sure that they've made the right decision and that they'll continue to be very happy together, that is, provided that Carol doesn't find out about last night!

Anyway, I think I've already said more than enough, so I'd just like to finish by wishing Martin and Carol every happiness for the future and by proposing the first toast, which is to the three beautiful bridesmaids, Christine, Jo and Sophie: the bridesmaids!"

13

ANALYSIS

Linking ideas

In his speech Ian uses a variety of words or phrases to introduce the different things that he says. These words are underlined in the first paragraph.

Below is a list of the different things that Ian says in each of the following four paragraphs.

Write the word or phrase which he uses to introduce each one in the spaces provided.

Paragraph 2

1	....	This morning I honestly thought that Martin might be too ill to come to the wedding.
2	....	I assumed that it was probably just an attack of nerves.
3	....	Martin didn't feel so bad after a cold shower and a lot of black coffee.
4	....	Please don't tell Carol about what Martin did last night.

Paragraph 3

5	....	I was so surprised when I heard that Martin and Carol had decided to get married.
6	....	Martin and Carol hadn't really had enough time to discover if they were really suited.
7	....	I said that I thought it would be more sensible to wait until they knew each other better before deciding to get married.

Paragraph 4

8	....	I'm delighted that Martin didn't take my advice and that they have got married at last.

Paragraph 5

9	....	My speech has already gone on too long.

PRACTICE

Exercise 1

First read the following speech, which was made at the leaving party for one of the directors of an advertising agency, and then fill in the gaps with suitable words, phrases or expressions from the list below.

Note that some of the items in the list can be used more than once.

SPEECH 2

.... , if I could just .... for a few minutes. Thank you. .... , the reason we're here today is to say 'Goodbye' to an old friend who's been with Sturrock and Mckay longer than most of us can remember.

.... , I'd just like to say a few words about her remarkable career at Sturrock and McKay. Well, believe it or not, Mary joined the company soon after the war, in 1946, ... that means that she has worked continuously for us for over forty years, which makes her easily the longest serving employee in the history of the company. .... , although she joined us as a secretary it wasn't long before her creative talents were recognised and during the next eighteen years she was promoted seven times until, finally, in 1964 she had become Artistic Director at the age of only thirty-five.

Over the last twenty-three years she has been one of the most dynamic people in the company and has worked extremely hard to establish Sturrock and Mckay as one of the top five agencies in the UK.

.... , I would like to .... contributing to the phenomenal success which we have enjoyed since the mid 1960s. .... , on behalf of everyone at Sturrock and Mckay I .... wish you .... in the future.

.... , ... to present you with this small token of our appreciation, which I hope will remind you of all your friends here during your long and well-deserved retirement, so I would like to .... , and if you'll all raise your glasses I'd like you to drink to Mary's health and happiness: Mary!

---

propose a toast　well　therefore　it gives me great pleasure　thank (you) for
would like to　now　first　right　anyway　every possible happiness
as you know　finally　have your attention　so

13

GUIDED WRITING

Composition task

First read the following exam question and then write a speech of between 120 and 180 words, using the structure suggested below.

> It is your last day at school. All of the students in your class have passed an important exam and you are celebrating with your teacher, who did an excellent job in preparing you all for the exam. You have been chosen by the class to present your teacher with a small gift.

SPEECH 3

Paragraph 1	Ask the other students to give you their attention and then remind them of the reason for this celebration.
Paragraph 2	Remind your classmates how difficult you all thought the exam was going to be **before** you took it and how worried everybody was about it. Say that as the course progressed you all began to feel more confident of passing.
Paragraph 3	Thank your teacher for all his/her hard work and excellent teaching in getting you ready for the exam.
Paragraph 4	Give him/her the present you have bought and say that you hope it will remind him/her of your class.

ANALYSIS

Text organisation

The sentences in the talk below are in the wrong order.

In pairs, put them in the correct order (1–12) and decide where the talk should be divided into paragraphs.

TALK 1

a Anyway, according to the story, the stain, which was apparently caused by the spilling of the unfortunate Earl's blood, was impossible to remove, no matter how many times the wall was washed. ☐

b Now, does anyone have any questions before we move on to the next room? ☐

c Good morning, ladies and gentlemen, and welcome to Collingwood Castle. ☐

d First, I'd like to draw your attention to these beautiful fifteenth century tapestries, which give us an idea of what life was like in the castle during the reign of Philip the Third. ☐

e Apparently, it marks the spot where the Earl of Beauchamp was killed in a duel by his wife's lover. ☐

f My name is Annette and I'm going to be your guide for the next hour or so. ☐

g This magnificent room, which is sixty metres long and thirty metres wide, was the place where the king received important guests, held meetings with his advisers and, of course, entertained members of the court to banquets and balls. ☐

h Finally, I'd just like to point out that the suit of armour hanging on the wall above the fireplace is from the late fifteenth century. ☐

i Now, before we start I'd like to ask you to save any questions you may have about each place we see until after I have finished speaking, so as not to waste too much time. ☐

j Next, I'd like to tell you a fascinating little story about this rather strange-looking stain on the wall behind me. ☐

k Right, as you can see, the room we are standing in is the Great Hall. ☐

l In fact, it was worn by Philip himself at the famous Battle of Sexton Moor. ☐

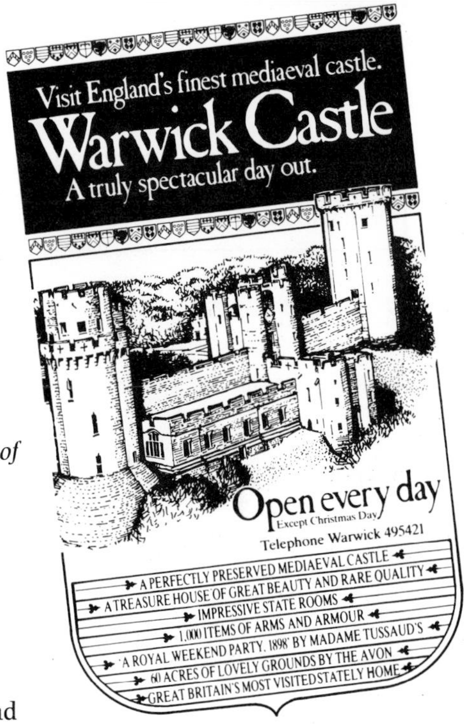

GUIDED WRITING

Composition task

Imagine that you are a tourist guide and that you are showing a group of visitors around a particularly interesting building in your country.

Write what you say to the group, using the structure suggested below and writing between 120 and 180 words.

TALK 2

Paragraph 1	Greet the group and welcome them to the place which they are going to visit. Introduce yourself and explain what the visit includes and how long it should take. Say if there is anything you should tell them or warn them about before you begin the visit.
Paragraph 2	Give the group some background information about the building, e.g. when it was built; who built it; how long it took to build; the style of the architecture; why it is famous.
Paragraph 3	Draw their attention to a particularly interesting feature, e.g. a tower, a window, a door, a mosaic, a painting.
Paragraph 4	Tell them an interesting story or anecdote connected with the building or a part of it, e.g. a murder, a quarrel, a drama, a famous incident.
Paragraph 5	Ask your group if they have any questions.

14 Essays on prescribed texts

PRESENTATION

First read the information on the right about 'Nineteen Eighty-Four' and then read the essay below, which describes the events leading to Winston and Julia's secret meeting in the country.

ESSAY 1

> GEORGE ORWELL: *Nineteen Eighty-Four*
> Describe the events leading to the afternoon on which Winston and Julia meet secretly in the country outside London.

One morning Winston is walking along a corridor in The Ministry of Truth, where he works, when a girl with her arm in a sling falls down in front of him. When he helps her to her feet she secretly slips a folded piece of paper into his hand and then continues on her way.

At first he thinks that it is either a message from the dreaded Thought Police or, perhaps, from some kind of illegal underground organisation. However, it is not until later on, when he is sure that he is not being watched, that he dares to unfold the piece of paper and read the message which is written on it. To his astonishment, it says, 'I love you.'

About a week later Winston finally manages to talk to Julia alone in the canteen for a few seconds and they quickly arrange to meet. That evening, after work, Winston and Julia meet in one of the main squares in London, Victory Square, where they are able to talk more freely. This is because the noise of the crowd, who are watching a convoy of Eurasian prisoners, makes it impossible for their conversation to be overheard by the telescreens. As the trucks carrying the prisoners pass by, Julia gives Winston instructions to meet her on the following Sunday in a hiding-place which she has discovered in the countryside not far from London.

That Sunday afternoon Winston catches a train to a small village outside London and walks into the countryside, where he meets Julia at the beginning of a narrow footpath which leads to the hiding-place in the middle of a wood.

Penguin Modern Classics

George Orwell

Nineteen Eighty-Four

1984 is the year in which it happens. The world is divided into three great powers, Oceania, Eurasia, and Eastasia, each perpetually at war with the other. Throughout Oceania 'The Party' rules by the agency of four ministries, whose power is absolute – the Ministry of Peace which deals with war, the Ministry of Love (headquarters of the dreaded Thought Police) which deals with law and order, the Ministry of Plenty which deals in scarcities, and the Ministry of Truth which deals with propaganda. The authorities keep a check on every action, word, gesture, or thought.

George Orwell's satire has been compared with that of Swift, and in *Nineteen Eighty-Four* the satire is the framework for one of the most moving stories to have been published in this generation – the human story of Winston Smith and his revolt against the Party's rule.

ANALYSIS

Text organisation

There are four paragraphs in the description of the events leading to Winston and Julia's meeting in the country.
Complete the following summary of each paragraph.

Paragraph 1 First, the writer describes the incident in which Julia .... and ....

Paragraph 2 Then he/she explains that Winston is extremely surprised when he .... because ....

Paragraph 3 Next he/she tells us that, a week later, Winston and Julia arrange to meet after work in Victory Square because ....

Paragraph 4 Finally, ...

Describing plot

1 *First, read the following extract from 'Nineteen Eighty-Four', in which Orwell describes how Julia deliberately falls over in front of Winston so that she can give him her message.*

> A solitary figure was coming towards him from the other end of the long, brightly-lit corridor ... As she came nearer he saw that her right arm was in a sling ... They were perhaps four metres apart when the girl stumbled and fell almost flat on her face ... Winston stopped short ... She held out her free hand to him, and he helped her up ... in the two or three seconds while he was helping her up the girl had slipped something into his hand ... It was a scrap of paper folded into a square.

Now compare the extract with the first paragraph of Essay 1, where the writer gives an account of the above incident in his/her own words.

What do you notice about the verbs which the writer uses in his/her composition?

2 *Using Orwell's original words, re-write the whole of the extract above as if you were giving a description of the incident in an essay. Make any changes to the tenses of the verbs which you think are necessary.*

Linking ideas

Using the underlined words to help you, complete the following sentences about Essay 1.

1 Winston works at ....

2 On the piece of paper Julia has written .... It says, 'I love you.'

3 Winston and Julia can speak together without fear of being overheard in .... because the crowd are making a lot of noise.

4 Most of the people in the square are ....

5 Julia knows where there is a good .... in the country near London.

6 That Sunday Winston meets Julia in .... outside London.

7 They walk down a narrow footpath to ....

PRACTICE

Exercise 1

*First read the following essay, which deals with a later episode in 'Nineteen Eighty-Four'. Then write each of the verbs in brackets in its correct tense and fill in the remaining gaps with a suitable relative pronoun (**who**, **where** or **which**).*

ESSAY 2

Describe how Winston and Julia are arrested by the Thought Police.

One evening Winston and Julia (be) (1) together in the little room .... (2) they (rent) (3) above a junk shop in a part of London .... (4) most of the houses are slums. Nobody, apart from O'Brien, (know) (5) about this room, ... (6) is a relatively safe hiding-place .... (7) Winston and Julia (meet) (8) once or twice a week for the last two months. There they (make) (9) love, (drink) (10) real coffee with real sugar and (enjoy) (11) each other's company for a couple of precious hours before returning separately to their homes.

Winston (be) (12) very excited because he (receive) (13) a copy of the forbidden book by Goldstein, ... (14) (be) (15) the leader of a subversive underground organisation. He (start) (16) reading extracts from the book to Julia but she (be) (17) too tired to concentrate and (fall) (18) asleep. Winston (finish) (19) the chapter .... (20) he (read) (21) and (fall) (22) asleep beside her.

Later, the two lovers (talk) (23) together when, suddenly, a voice from behind a picture on the wall (order) (24) them to stand in the middle of the room with their hands behind their heads. The picture (fall) (25) off the wall and they (see) (26) that behind it there (be) (27) a telescreen, ... (28) (listen) (29) to all of their conversations.

At that moment several uniformed members of the Thought Police (burst) (30) into the room and violently (arrest) (31) them. To Winston's amazement, the policemen (be) (32) accompanied by Mr Charrington, ... (33) (own) (34) the junk shop below, and Winston (realise) (35) that he (be) (36) also a member of the Thought Police.

GUIDED WRITING

Composition task

ESSAY 3

Using Essay 1 and Essay 2 to help you, give a description of an important episode in a novel or play (or film) that you know well. You should write between 120 and 180 words.

PRESENTATION

Read the following essay, in which the writer describes the character of Romeo, from Shakespeare's 'Romeo and Juliet'.

ESSAY 4

WILLIAM SHAKESPEARE: *Romeo and Juliet*
Describe the character of Romeo.

At the beginning of the play Romeo is rather sad and miserable because he is in love with Rosaline but she does not return his love. His friends Benvolio and Mercutio, who are much more interested in physical love than spiritual love, tell him not to take love so seriously. Therefore, it is clear right from the start that, unlike his friends, Romeo is a romantic character who has a pure, idealistic attitude towards love.

Later we see that Romeo is an extremely impulsive young man, someone who takes decisions on the spur of the moment, without considering the consequences of his actions. For example, he foolishly decides to climb up the side of the Capulets' house to Juliet's balcony, in spite of the fact that their families are sworn enemies and that the Capulets would surely kill him if they found him there. What is more, Romeo immediately decides to marry Juliet, even though they have only known each other for a few hours and despite the fact that their families would never agree to the marriage. This also shows that Romeo is a highly emotional, passionate young man whose actions are ruled by his heart rather than by his head.

Another side of Romeo's character is his courage. This is revealed when he bravely fights and kills Tybalt in a duel to defend his family's honour after the latter has killed Mercutio.

Finally, Romeo is a tragic character. He has a fatalistic attitude towards the events in his life and is convinced that he has absolutely no control over his own destiny. For example, he accepts unquestioningly that it is his fate to fall in love with Juliet and to marry her, even after he discovers that she is a Capulet. Another example of his willingness to accept his destiny is when he receives the news of Juliet's 'death' and immediately decides to buy the poison so that he can die with her.

ANALYSIS

Text organisation

Complete the following notes about the essay above.

ROMEO – A CHARACTER STUDY

	Qualities	Evidence
Paragraph 1	romantic	unhappy at beginning of play because Ros. does not return his love
	idealistic	wants spiritual love, not just physical love
Paragraph 2	impulsive	.... , in spite of danger
	....	decides to marry J. although they hardly know each other and their
	....	families would oppose marriage
Paragraph 3	brave	....
Paragraph 4	....	accepts that it is his fate to fall in love with J. and marry her
	....	....
		....

GUIDED WRITING

Essay planning

Write notes like those above for an essay in which you examine a character from a novel or play (or film) that you know well.

QUALITIES	EVIDENCE
....	....
....	....
....	....
....	....
....	....

Composition task

ESSAY 5

Using the notes you have made above, write an essay describing the character of one of the chief protagonists of a novel or play (or film) that you know well. You should write between 120 and 180 words.